KNITTED BEADED
JEWELRY

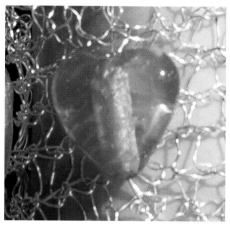

KNITTED BEADED JEWELRY

16 Stylish Projects for Jewelry & Accessories

Ruth Herring

STACKPOLE
BOOKS

Originally published in 2008 by
    New Holland Publishers (UK) Ltd.

Published by
STACKPOLE BOOKS
5067 Ritter Road
Mechanicsburg, PA 17055
www.stackpolebooks.com

Printed in Singapore

10 9 8 7 6 5 4 3 2 1

First edition

Senior Editor: Naomi Waters
Designer: Lisa Tai
Main photography: Paul West
Models: Anouck Boungnang, Sarah Green, and Josie Evetts
Step-by-step photography: Shona Wood
Production: Hema Gohil
Editorial Direction: Rosemary Wilkinson

Cover design by Caroline Stover

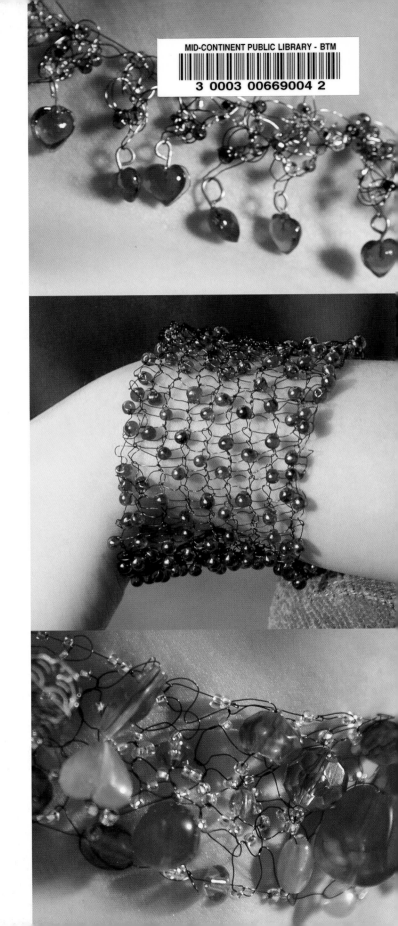

Contents

Introduction

During my long career as a knitwear designer, I have been asked to undertake many interesting projects, including hand-knitted versions of the Mona Lisa, Michaelangelo's David, and the album cover of The Beatles' Abbey Road. Without computer-aided design, these projects really stretched my drawing and pattern-drafting skills to the limit. It raises the question, "Is Dan Brown smart enough to crack a Da Vinci knitting pattern?"—I don't think so!

Fifteen years on, these commissions seem tame compared to the fun "knitted wedding" and (maybe) less appropriate knitted "willy warmers"—created by UK-based urban knitters Cast Off—all in the name of art. At the couture end, John Galliano's full-scale ball gown knitted with intricate cables is a masterpiece of technical expertise—definitely a piece fit for a gallery.

There is very little that isn't re-created in knitted form these days—a knitted Ferrari and a knitted garden both made the news in 2007. The truth is that knitting is fun and an extremely versatile craft, enabling you to attempt wonderful creations, such as the jewelry and accessories featured in this book.

These projects have been designed to suit most tastes and skill levels. If you are a beginner, the techniques section will guide you through the knitting process, and the patterns are star-coded for you to identify the patterns to attempt first. You'll be surprised that some of the most striking are often the simplest to make. The beauty of knitted jewelry is it doesn't break the bank—a few beads and some wire or thread and you are ready.

Enjoy!

MATERIALS, EQUIPMENT AND TECHNIQUES

1 materials and equipment

Unlike some knitting projects, making jewelry and small accessories won't break the bank. Small spools of craft wire or crochet thread are inexpensive and will provide enough material to complete several items. Apart from knitting needles, most of the equipment can be found in your sewing box or toolbox.

2 techniques

You don't have to be an expert knitter to attempt many of the stunning projects in this book. Learn to cast on and bind off to produce a sparkly bracelet and earring set, or master stockinette stitch to knit a truly glamorous choker scattered with tiny glass pendant beads. More challenging projects are the Aran knitting items—a pretty embroidered wristband or a neat little bag featuring shaping techniques.

Materials

The choice of materials used in a project plays a huge part in the overall design process. Try transforming a few basic knitting stitches into something special with some pretty beads and a spool of thread or wire, or experiment with contrasting or coordinating materials to create different effects.

Beads

Hunting for beads can be a daunting and bewildering task, with suppliers' catalogs listing beads under different categories and manufacturers using a range of names for the finishes on their beads. Here is a list of some of the more common beads available, with a description to help you identify them.

SEED BEADS AND ROCAILLES

Seed beads and rocailles are essentially the same thing—small glass beads that can be used for beading, embroidery, and fine knitting and crochet. The only noticeable difference is that rocailles have a square hole, while seed beads have a round hole, which is often silver-lined (see Bead Finishes, page 12).

Seed beads are manufactured in India, Japan, Taiwan, and the Czech Republic and have slightly different characteristics, depending on their country of origin. Generally speaking, the Czech beads are more rounded, while beads from Asia and the Pacific have more cylindrical shapes. Japanese beads are more regular in shape than those from Taiwan, while Indian beads are the most irregularly shaped.

Seed beads are sized by number—the smaller the number, the larger the bead. The smallest seed beads used in the projects in this book are size 10/0, which are worked with fine wire, and the largest, size 5/0, are used with 1 mm leather cord.

BUGLE BEADS

Bugle beads are lengths of cut-glass cane available in sizes ranging from 2 mm to 30 mm. Bugle beads can be used with wire and with threads up to 4-ply in thickness. If using them with thread, the bugle beads will need to be threaded using the threading bead technique for threads, which is demonstrated on page 25.

PONY BEADS

These are like large seed beads in shape and are made in glass, plastic, or wood. They are normally available in two sizes: 7 x 4 mm and 9 x 6 mm and are ideal for use with thicker yarns and more unusual materials such as raffia, ribbon, and plastic laces. Plastic pony beads are inexpensive and are great for trying out ideas and techniques before moving on to using more costly glass beads. Great stocking fillers for children, pony beads are available in different finishes such as "glow in the dark," "sparkle," and "neon."

PRESSED GLASS BEADS

Usually large in size, these are molded beads that form unusual shapes and make a real statement in any piece. They are available in many beautiful finishes, some of the best being silver-lined and color-lined (see Bead Finishes, page 12).

PENDANT BEADS

Any bead that has the hole pierced through the top, which allows it to dangle, is described as a pendant bead. They come in many different guises.

WIRED PENDANT BEADS

Adding wires to different-shaped glass beads produces pretty pendant shapes, which add movement to a jewelry piece.

FACETED BEADS

These are glass or plastic, hand- or machine-cut beads. Their distinctive multiple flat faces catch the light and give the beads an extra sparkle. Faceted beads are available in many different finishes and shapes, including bicones, hearts, and teardrops. The prettiest finish is an iridescent (AB) finish (see Bead Finishes, page 12), which adds extra sparkle when combined with the faceted edges.

SEED BEADS

PRESSED GLASS BEADS

FACETED BEADS

BUGLE BEADS

PENDANT BEADS

VENETIAN GLASS BEADS

SEQUINS

DISCS

PONY BEADS

WIRED PENDANTS

VENETIAN GLASS BEADS

Venetian beads are intended to dazzle the eye and are often lavishly decorated—making them unlike any other beads in the world. Each original Venetian bead is handmade and it is almost impossible to describe all the different types, but one thing is for sure—they are spectacular! Many feature vibrant colors that glimmer beneath 24ct gold or silver foil, while others have gold leaf applied directly to the surface. There are also beads made with aventurine, a special glass paste composed with copper flakes, or plain glass beads enhanced with a trail of molten glass in a second color dribbled across the surface. The Fiorato bead is created using melted glass to hand-paint flowers and decorations.

SEQUINS AND DISCS

These are made from pressed pieces of thin plastic and are available in a variety of colors, shapes, and sizes. The main difference between a disc and a sequin is the former has a hole at the top, whereas a sequin has a hole in its center.

Degrees of Bead Transparency

Glass beads come in various degrees of transparency.

Transparent or clear: Beads transmit light and are, therefore, easy to see through even when they are coloured. They are available in many colors and are sometimes lined (see Bead Finishes, below).

Translucent: You cannot see clearly through a translucent glass bead.

Opal: Replicating the look of an opal gemstone, these beads transmit light with the milky, translucent effect produced by the addition of fluorides to the molten glass.

Opaque: This is the name for glass beads that you cannot see through.

Bead Finishes

Once the transparency has been selected, the bead can have a range of finishes added, as described below.

Color-lined: These beads are made with transparent glass with the inside of the hole dyed or painted with an opaque color. The resulting effect is a greatly enhanced bead color.

Silver-lined: Silver-lined beads have a mirrorlike reflective lining in their holes to enhance the color of the bead. Beads with silver-lined square holes (often called rocailles) reflect the light even more.

Luster: The term luster describes a clear, uniform, and shiny finish given to transparent, opal, or opaque beads. The well-known term "pearlized" is given to an opaque luster bead, and opal-lusted beads are also known as "Ceylon."

Satin: The shade of a satin bead will change, depending on how the bead is viewed; a white satin bead will have a distinctive gray shade on one side. The layers or striations are due to the many air bubbles created in its molten stage. The finish has a sheen instead of being overtly shiny, giving it an expensive look.

Iridescent: Also known as iris, irid, rainbow, aurora borealis (AB), and scarab(ee), these beads are best described as having an "oil slick"-type finish. Fuming metal salts onto the hot glass to form a permanent bond creates this finish.

Metallic or galvanized: This describes beads given a shiny, metal-like surface coating. Unlike the iridescent finish, this surface is not permanent because it is normally a baked-on paint. When purchasing these types of beads, check the manufacturer's recommendations if the finished piece is to be washed or will become wet at any time.

Mat metallic: As for metallic, but the finish has a flat instead of a shiny look.

Mat or frosted: This is the name given to a bead with a dull or flat finish. The frosted finish will have a distinctive icy appearance.

DK AND 4-PLY YARNS

CROCHET
THREAD

FANCY YARN

WIRE

1 MM
CORD

2 MM
CORD

Wire and yarns

WIRE

Working with wire has become increasingly popular over the past few years, with craft wires now available in a wide range of colors and thicknesses.

Wire is measured in millimeters or by the American Wire Gauge (AWG) and craft wire is available from size 2.05 mm (12 AWG) to the fine 0.100 mm (38 AWG). All the wire projects in this book are worked in 0.20 mm (32 AWG) craft wire or silver-plated copper wire, with the exception of the Chunky glass wristbands (see page 80), which are knitted in thick 0.50 mm (24 AWG) silver-plated or black wire.

YARNS

Cotton and cotton-mix yarns are available in many colors in both 4-ply and DK. Color ranges become more limited with thicker yarns such as Aran and chunky, but sometimes a good source is a machine-knitting supplier that will sell yarns on the cone. If finer yarn is needed, crochet threads are beautiful to knit with on smaller needles, such as 2 mm needles. Crochet threads can be expensive because they are often very good quality, but one ball is sufficient to make many of the wristbands featured in this book. For real luxury, try substituting with a fine silk thread—again these can be purchased from good outlets and machine-knitting suppliers.

WOOL AND SYNTHETIC YARNS

Some knitters don't like knitting with cotton yarn and prefer something with a bit more spring. Wool, wool mixes, and synthetics such as acrylic are available in a wide range of thicknesses, colors, and textures to suit all budgets. Some of the wonderful fancy yarns on the market are fun—experiment with ribbon or slub yarns to create unusual effects.

LEATHER CORD

Leather cord makes a great alternative to knitting yarn when a simple chunky design is to be knitted. Round leather cord is best for knitting and it can be found in 1 mm and 2 mm thicknesses and a selection of beautiful natural shades. If you don't wear leather, there are fantastic substitutes in the form of waxed cotton cords.

Findings

The word "finding" is a generic term used to cover all the connectors and closures used to complete jewelry pieces. Hooks and clasps are available in a huge range of sizes and finishes, with some of the finest replicating antique styles. They can be used effectively to enhance knitted jewelry and some of the most popular findings are illustrated here.

LOBSTER CLASPS

These are used to fasten necklaces and bracelets and are available in a variety of styles. To fasten, they are normally used in conjunction with a jump ring or a necklace connector.

HOOKS

Hooks are often purchased as sets with a loop to match. They can be found in a wide range of sizes, designs, and finishes with one of the most popular being the Shepherd's Crook Hook.

TOGGLE CLASPS

A two-piece closure, a bar is inserted sideways into a clasp, which has a diameter smaller than the width of the bar to keep it in place. The clasp element is often round, but they can be found in a variety of shapes including square, heart, and oval. They are popular as closures for loose bracelets and necklaces and are available in a wide range of sizes and finishes.

END CONNECTORS

These are ideal for fastening wide pieces of jewelry because they work as a transition between the piece and the clasp. Available in a range of widths and finishes, they can be purchased as adjustable sets with a chain and lobster clasp.

CHAIN

Adding a length of chain to the closure creates an adjustable piece of jewelry—perfect when the piece is to be worn as a tight choker. Use single-link chain large enough to use a lobster clasp as a closure. A beaded head pin or eye pin can be added to finish a raw end (see Hearts necklace page 69).

BOX CLASPS

Made up of two pieces, one slipping into the other, these are perfect for small items, such as bracelets. Again, they can be found in a wide variety of sizes and finishes.

MAGNETIC CLASPS

If fastening jewelry is problematic, try substituting the closure with a magnetic clasp. They can be used in pairs if the jewelry piece is heavy, but they are perfect for lightweight jewelry.

CONES AND END CAPS

Cones and end caps, also called bead caps, are available in many styles for finishing raw ends of necklaces and bracelets. They work well in conjunction with toggle clasps to produce ornate closures (see Seed-bead cotton bracelets, page 54).

JUMP RINGS

These are small metal circles of wire, which are available in a variety of sizes for connecting findings. They are attached by opening them laterally, instead of pulling them apart, which weakens the metal.

NECKLACE CONNECTORS

These are used in conjunction with a clasp. The smaller hole is for attaching the finding; the larger hole becomes the fastener.

EARRING WIRES

These are suitable for pierced ears and are available in slightly different shapes, one of the most elegant and popular being the fish-hook wire. Different types of screw or clasp fittings are available for those without piercings. Whichever style you opt for, be careful of allergies if you are giving earrings as a gift— sterling silver is possibly the safest option.

CALOTTES

Also known as damshell crimp, these act as a transition between the thread and the metal finding. They secure and cover knots and crimp beads at the end of a necklace, bracelet, or earring. The knot or crimp bead is placed into the calotte, which is gently squeezed closed with a pair of flat-nosed pliers. The calotte can be secured to the finding with a jump ring.

HEAD PIN AND EYE PIN

A head pin is a straight piece of wire with a small perpendicular disc at one end. Beads can be threaded on and the remaining wire used to attach to a finding or chain end. The eye pin has a small loop end for attaching wired pendants (see Hearts necklace, page 69).

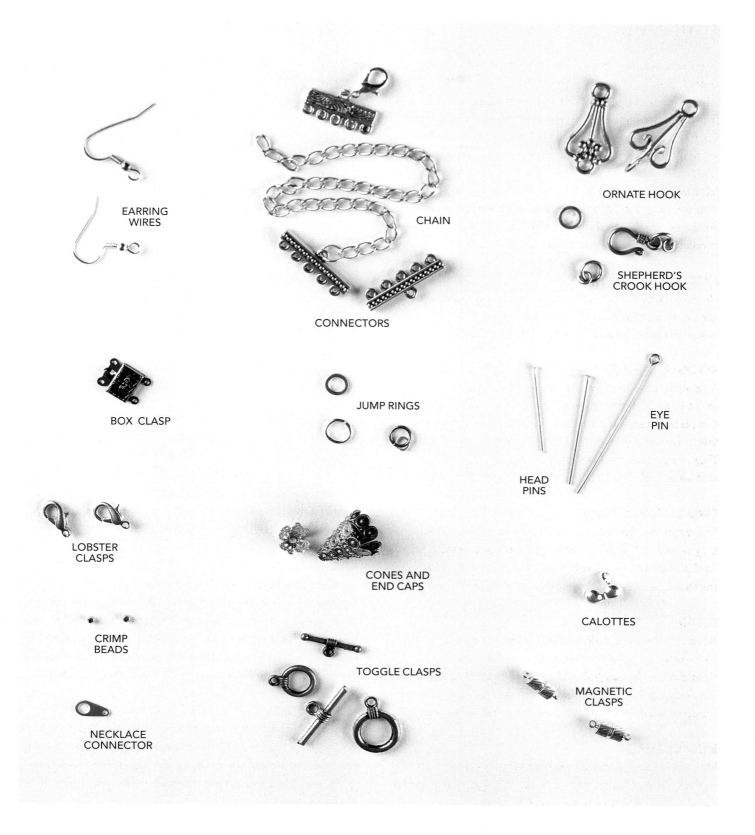

EARRING WIRES

CHAIN

ORNATE HOOK

CONNECTORS

SHEPHERD'S CROOK HOOK

BOX CLASP

JUMP RINGS

EYE PIN

HEAD PINS

LOBSTER CLASPS

CONES AND END CAPS

CALOTTES

CRIMP BEADS

TOGGLE CLASPS

MAGNETIC CLASPS

NECKLACE CONNECTOR

Equipment

It is easy to get started in knitting with just a couple of pairs of needles, a knitters' sewing needle, and some balls of yarn. Working with wire adds a few more pieces of equipment to the tool kit, which can also be used for other jewelry making.

KNITTING NEEDLES

Modern knitting needles are made from aluminum, plastic, wood, or bamboo. Older needles were also made of anodized aluminum, tortoiseshell, bone, ivory, celluloid, and even silver. Knitting needles come in pairs and a variety of lengths, and the needle tip should taper to a blunt point.

CABLE NEEDLES

A cable needle is the third, shorter needle used to create cable stitches. They can be straight, like small double-pointed needles, or have a bend in the middle, which helps to stop the stitches from falling off during the cable process. Less common is the "fish-hook" shape, which again holds the stitches safely.

NEEDLE GAUGE

The needle-size chart (see left) will help to convert sizes of needles, but if you have a pair of needles with no indication of size, for example, circular needles, check the size by pushing the needle into the holes on a gauge. The correct needle size is indicated by the smallest hole that the needle fits through.

KNITTING NEEDLE SIZE

The needle-size chart (see left) chart will give the conversions for British, European, and American needle sizes. British imperial needles (pre-metric) are still widely available secondhand in the United Kingdom.

ROUND-NOSE PLIERS

To avoid the surface of the wire being spoiled, the pliers used for wirework jewelry do not have teeth like conventional types. Round-nose pliers are used for gripping and bending wire—they have round, tight jaws that taper to a point.

FLAT-NOSE PLIERS

These have tapered jaws with a flat inside edge. They are used for opening and closing jump rings and for squeezing crimp beads. Lightweight, smooth-jawed pliers avoid damaging the wire. Flat-nose pliers with angled heads are also available. Use a pair of each type for joining small jump rings to connectors.

SIDE CUTTERS

Also known as flush cutters, the cutting end has a flat side and an angled side. The flat side is positioned against the work for a straight close cut. The blade is very sharp to avoid burring or marking the metal. Choose a small, lightweight pair for jewelry making.

European Metric	British Metric	Imperial	USA
2.00 mm	2.00 mm	14	0
–	2¼ mm	13	1
2.50 mm	–	–	–
–	2¾ mm	12	2
3.00 mm	3.00 mm	11	–
–	3¼ mm	10	3
3.50 mm	–	–	4
–	3¾ mm	9	5
4.00 mm	4.00 mm	8	6
4.50 mm	4½ mm	7	7
5.00 mm	5.00 mm	6	8
5.50 mm	5½ mm	5	9
6.00 mm	6.00 mm	4	10
6.50 mm	6½ mm	3	10½
7.00 mm	7.00 mm	2	–
7.50 mm	7½ mm	1	–
8.00 mm	8.00 mm	0	11
9.00 mm	9.00 mm	00	13
10.00 mm	10.00 mm	000	15

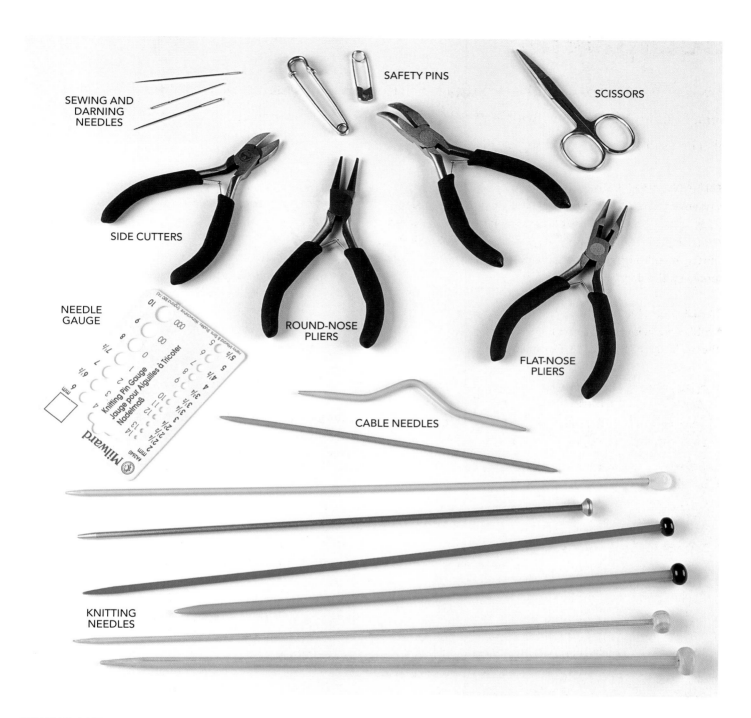

SEWING AND
DARNING
NEEDLES

SAFETY PINS

SCISSORS

SIDE CUTTERS

ROUND-NOSE
PLIERS

FLAT-NOSE
PLIERS

NEEDLE
GAUGE

Knitting Pin Gauge
Jauge pour Aiguilles à Tricoter
Nadelmaß

Milward

CABLE NEEDLES

KNITTING
NEEDLES

SEWING AND DARNING NEEDLES

A selection of different sizes and types of sewing needles are an essential part of a knitter's tool kit. "Knitter's needles" have a blunt end for sewing seams without splitting the yarn, while for darning in tail ends a pointed needle is used because the yarn is split during the darning process. Small-eyed needles are used for threading on seed beads. See Sewing on Beads on page 32.

SAFETY PINS

A collection of safety pins is a useful addition to a tool kit. They are useful for holding stitches and as markers.

Techniques

Learning just a few basic stitches will open up a whole new and useful set of skills. Refer to the abbreviations on page 33 whenever needed to familiarize yourself with the knitting terms.

Holding the needles

Basic knitting stitches are worked on two needles. There is no right or wrong way to hold the needles, so simply pick up a pair of needles to find a comfortable hold. However, two main needle holds can be identified as follows:

PEN HOLD
Better suited to shorter needles because the RH needle is supported by the right hand and wrist.

The RH needle is held in the crux of the RH thumb like a pen. The LH needle is held in an overhand position.

KNIFE HOLD
The RH needle can be supported under the arm, allowing the needle to be released as the yarn is wound to make a stitch.

Also known as the overhand grip, the RH needle is held like a knife, with the LH needle held as for the pen hold. The knife hold is better for longer needles.

Holding the yarn

Again, this is very personal to each knitter and it is best to experiment until a hold is found that suits you. The aim is for the yarn to feed evenly during knitting, making each stitch the same size. Here are some popular yarn holds:

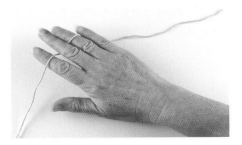

Feed the yarn over the index finger, under the middle finger, and over the third finger, finishing by gripping the yarn a bit more securely with the pinkie.

Feed as in the first example, but wind the yarn around the pinkie to create a firmer tension.

Hold the yarn firmly between the thumb and index finger of the right hand. This provides great control over the tension of the stitches, especially when working with wire.

Basic stitches

The following section outlines all the basic stitches that are used to make the projects in this book. If you are a beginner, start with some inexpensive yarn to practice the stitches using these step-by-step instructions. Once the slip knot and one of the casting-on methods have been mastered, the knit and purl stitches—along with binding off—will be enough for you to attempt most of the projects featured in this book.

SLIP KNOT

To begin knitting, the first thing to be mastered is the slip knot. This will become the first stitch of any knitted piece.

① *Leaving enough tail end for attaching findings, place the end of the yarn in the palm of the hand and hold in place with the bottom two fingers. Straighten the index and middle fingers and wind the yarn over and around them, crossing the yarn at the front of the fingers.*

② *Still holding the tail end in place, make a scissors with the top two fingers and push a loop through from the back.*

③ *Take the top two fingers out of the loop and pull the loop and the tail end gently until a knot is formed. The loop can be made smaller by pulling the yarn from the spool end.*

CASTING ON

The next step in knitting is casting on some stitches. There are many different methods, but here are two of the most useful. The loop cast on is used for a loose edge, and the cable cast on for a firm edge.

LOOP CAST ON

This is the most basic cast-on stitch, just requiring one knitting needle and your thumb. As it is simple to work, it is a better method for thicker wires. The stitches can be formed to any tension, but be careful to pull each stitch to the same tension.

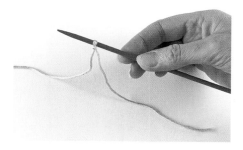

① *Leaving a tail end, make a slip knot and place on the needle. Hold the needle in the right hand.*

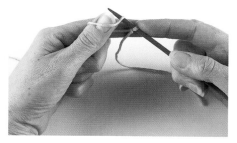

② *Make a loop around the left thumb and place on the needle.*

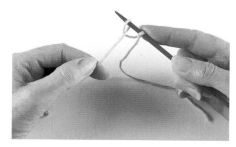

③ *Slip the thumb out and gently pull to the desired tension.*

CABLE CAST ON

This method creates a neat edge, ideal for pieces that require a firm and strong edge that is less likely to stretch. The technique is worked with two needles. Each stitch is given a twist as it is formed, giving the edge a distinctive cable look.

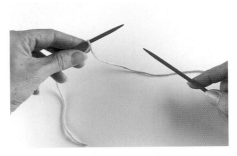
① *Make a slip knot and place loop on LH needle.*

② *Insert RH needle into the loop and cross the needle to back. Wrap the yarn around RH needle and between the needles.*

③ *Controlling the yarn, draw through a loop to about ¾ in length.*

④ *Bring the LH needle to the front and insert into the loop, placing the loop on the LH needle. Do not tighten the loop.*

⑤ *Insert RH needle between the two stitches on LH needle. Tighten the last stitch made.*

⑥ *Wrap the yarn around RH needle and between the needles. Repeat steps 3–6 to make the number of stitches you require.*

KNIT STITCH

① *With the yarn at the back of the work, insert the RH needle from left to right through the front of the next stitch on the LH needle.*

② *Wrap the yarn around the back of the RH needle and between the needles.*

③ *Controlling the yarn, draw through a loop to the front.*

④ *Slip the original stitch off the LH needle. Repeat steps 1–4 until all the stitches have been transferred to the RH needle.*

PURL STITCH

① *With the yarn at the front of the work, insert the RH needle from right to left through the front of the next stitch on the LH needle.*

② *Wrap the yarn between the needles and around to the front of the RH needle.*

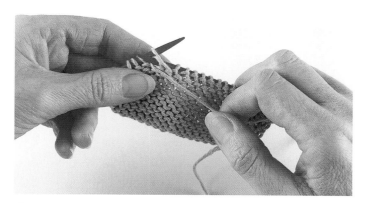

③ *Controlling the yarn, draw through a loop to the back.*

④ *Slip the original stitch off the LH needle. Repeat steps 1–4 until all the stitches have been transferred to the RH needle.*

Finishing off

A knitted piece remains unstable until the stitches have been bound off and the last stitch secured. Yarn is easy to unravel if corrections need to be made to the pattern and is less likely to spoil if it is unpicked soon after it is knitted. Wire does not easily unravel if you accidentally drop a stitch; however, it is less easy to unpick if mistakes have been made.

BINDING OFF

When binding off, try to keep to the pattern as it is set. For example, if the next row is a knit row, then use knit stitches for the bound-off row. Binding off in rib should always be worked as if continuing to rib.

① *Work the first two stitches of the row. Here, knit stitches have been used. * Using the LH needle, lift the first stitch knitted on the RH needle over the second stitch and drop it off the needle. Knit the next stitch and repeat from *.*

② *When the binding off is completed, leave a tail end and cut the yarn. Pass the end through the last loop and pull to fasten off. The tail end can be used for sewing on findings, joining the seam for a ring, or it can be darned into the work to neaten off.*

SEWING ON FINDINGS (YARN)

Oversew, but bear in mind that yarn is a lot thicker than wire, so it will not require as many stitches. Thicker yarn can be split for sewing the very small connector holes on some of the more delicate findings.

DARNING OFF TAIL ENDS (YARN)

Do not knot yarns together because ugly lumps are created and the knot may work loose over time. Always neaten off one tail end at a time by weaving in different directions to avoid excess thickness. Make sure that the stitches do not show on the right side of the work. Trim excess close to the work.

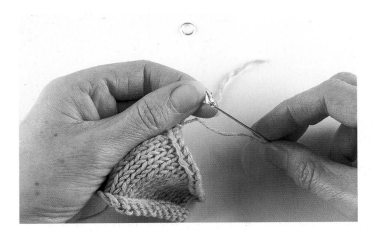

Sewing on findings

Darning off tail ends

SEWING ON FINDINGS (WIRE)

Always bear in mind that jump rings and ear wires have tiny gaps that will allow a single thread of wire to escape. When attaching findings, therefore, make four to five oversew stitches to secure.

DARNING OFF TAIL ENDS (WIRE)

To finish off tail ends, thread the tail end onto a large-eyed sewing needle and weave through the last row of the work. Threading the wire through any beads on the way will help to secure. Trim close to the work with side cutters.

Sewing on end connector using wire

Darning off wire tail ends

Knitted fabrics

After mastering casting on and binding off, along with knit and purl stitches, a range of knitted fabrics can be worked which form the basis of many of the projects in this book.

GARTER STITCH (g st)

Working every row in knit stitch produces garter stitch. This fabric is reversible and although it is the simplest of all the knitted fabrics, achieving an even tension takes a bit of practice.

STOCKINETTE STITCH (st.st)

The RS rows are worked in knit stitch; the WS rows in purl stitch. This fabric will curl if it is not bordered with garter stitch, seed stitch, or rib, but the curl can be used effectively (see page 54).

REVERSE STOCKINETTE STITCH (rev st.st)

Working the RS rows in purl and the WS rows in knit throughout produces reverse stockinette stitch. Reverse stockinette stitch will also curl if it is not bordered.

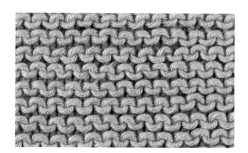

Garter stitch sample in DK yarn

Stockinette stitch sample in DK yarn

Reverse stockinette stitch sample

RIGHT AND WRONG SIDE OF ROWS (RS; WS)

A right side row is where the right side of the work is facing you as you work and a wrong side row is where the wrong side of the work is facing you. The instruction "ending with a wrong side row" means that the next row will be an RS row.

Knit-and-purl stitch patterns

Once garter stitch and stocking stitch are mastered, try using knit and purl stitches in the same row to produce ribbed and seed stitch fabrics. Other knit and purl patterns were popular in traditional British Guernsey and other "fisherman" sweaters. The pattern possibilities are endless, with many of the traditional designs being influenced by coastal scenery. Three of the most useful knit-and-purl patterns are shown here.

① *Knit 1 stitch then bring yarn between needles to the front of the work ready for the purl stitch.*

② *Purl next stitch then take yarn between needles to the back of work ready for the knit stitch.*

RIBBED STITCHES

The knit and purl stitches form verticals, creating an elastic fabric. Working these patterns on needles smaller than those used for most other knitted fabrics enhances the elasticity. Ribs are perfect for designs that require a close fit or for cuffs and edgings. These fabrics are reversible and do not curl.

SINGLE RIB

This is the most elastic rib. This pattern is worked over 1 or 2 rows, depending on the number of stitches cast on.

Worked over an odd number of stitches:
Row 1: K1 * p1, k1, rep from * to end.
Row 2: P1 * k1, p1, rep from * to end.
Rep rows 1 and 2 until desired length.
Worked over an even number of stitches:
Row 1: * K1, p1, rep from * to end.

Single rib

SEED STITCHES

These fabrics are reversible and do not curl, making them ideal for borders or all over patterns. They are commonly used in conjunction with cable and twist stitches in traditional Aran patterns. There are two types; seed stitch as used in the wristband and hairband (page 57) and double seed stitch, as used in the small Aran bag (page 90).

SEED STITCH

This pattern is worked over 1 or 2 rows, depending on the number of stitches cast on.

Worked over an odd number of stitches:
Row 1: K1 * p1, k1, rep from * to end.
Rep row 1 until desired length.
Worked over an even number of stitches:
Row 1: * K1, p1, rep from * to end.
Row 2: * P1, k1, rep from * to end.
Rep rows 1 and 2 until desired length.

Seed stitch

DOUBLE SEED STITCH
(Irish Seed Stitch)
Also known as Irish seed stitch, the pattern is worked over 4 rows.

Worked over an odd number of stitches:

Row 1: K1 * p1, k1, rep from * to end.
Row 2: P1 * k1, p1, rep from * to end.
Row 3: As row 2.
Row 4: As row 1.
Rep rows 1 to 4 until desired length.

Worked over an even number of stitches:

Row 1: * K1, p1, rep from * to end.
Row 2: As row 1.
Row 3: * P1, k1, rep from * to end.
Row 4: As row 3.
Rep rows 1 to 4 until desired length.

Double seed stitch

Knitting with beads

Adding beads to knitting is surprisingly easy. Beautiful bead combinations and simple stitches are all that are needed to create stunning designs. Most of the projects in this book require the beads to be strung onto the yarn before the knitting is started. Follow the bead set-up instructions for each project and, once the beads are threaded, make a slip knot to prevent the beads from sliding off before you start knitting.

THREADING BEADS ONTO WIRE
When working with wire the beads can be threaded straight onto the wire without the use of additional aids.

THREADING BEADS ONTO COTTON AND WOOL YARNS
Because these yarns are less rigid than wire, threading the beads requires the use of sewing needles. The size of the needle used will depend on the thickness of the yarn and the size of the beads to be threaded.

Pour the beads into a shallow dish, preferably one that doesn't have ridges in which small seed beads can get trapped. Make a very slight bend in the end of the wire and push the wire gently through the beads—the seed beads will just pop onto the wire!

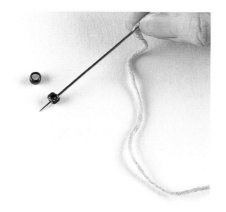

① If the beads to be used have large holes, thread the yarn straight onto a large-eyed knitter's sewing needle to string on enough beads to complete the project.

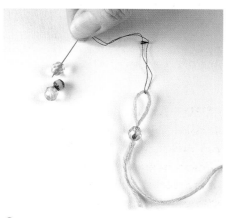

② For fine beads, thread a length (approx 4 in) of strong sewing thread through a small-eyed sewing needle. Tie the ends to make a loop. Pass the end of the knitting yarn through the loop. Use the sewing needle to pick up the beads and pull along the double thickness of yarn until it reaches the single thread.

SLIPPING BEADS

This is the easiest and most versatile way to work beads into knitting because, within reason, any shape bead can be knitted in. The size and shape of the bead will determine the number of stitches that are slipped at any one time. The thread bracelets on page 54 involve slipping just one stitch per bead, whereas the chunky glass beads used for the wristbands on page 80 require 5 stitches per bead to be slipped. The beads are worked on the RS of st.st.

① *Knit to the stitch where the bead is to be placed. Yfwd and bring up a bead and push close to RH needle. Slip the stitch purlwise.*

② *Keeping bead in place with left thumb, ybk and knit the next stitch.*

CASTING ON WITH BEADS

Some of the projects in this book require the beads to be knitted at the casting-on stage. This is straightforward, but remember when calculating the number of beads to thread, the slip knot will not be beaded.

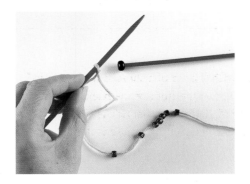

① *Thread onto the yarn the number of beads required, make a slip knot, and place on LH needle.*

② ** Insert RH needle into next stitch (or between stitches if working cable cast on), bring up a bead to the needle, and wrap the yarn around the needle.*

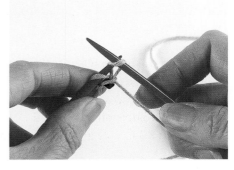

③ *Draw through a loop and place on the LH needle to form the next stitch. Rep from * until desired number of stitches have been worked.*

ADDING A BEAD ON A KNIT STITCH

Adding beads to a knit stitch forces the beads to the back of the stitch. Used in conjunction with a beaded purl row will create beaded rev st.st.

① *Bring up a bead and hold close to the RH needle. Insert the RH needle and wrap the yarn in a knitwise direction.*

② *Draw through a loop to the front. Slip the original stitch off the LH needle. The bead will lie at the back of the stitch.*

ADDING A BEAD ON A PURL STITCH

Adding beads to a purl stitch allows the beads to lie at the front of the stitch.

① Bring up a bead and hold close to the RH needle. Insert the RH needle in the next stitch and wrap the yarn in a purlwise direction.

② Draw through a loop to the back. Slip the original stitch off the LH needle. The bead will lie in the front of the stitch.

Cables

Cables are worked simply by changing the order in which groups of stitches are knitted with the aid of a short, double pointed cable needle (CN). Depending on whether the stitches moved onto the cable needle are held at the front or the back of the work the stitches will lie in a diagonal to the left or right. When a cable pattern is prefixed with "C," it means that all the stitches in the cable will be knitted. Simple two-stitch cables can be worked with or without a cable needle. The latter method is described on page 57, while the cable needle method is worked as follows:

C2B (Cable 2 Back) with CN

① Work to 1 stitch before the knit stitch to be cabled. Slip next stitch onto a CN, hold at the back, and knit the next stitch from the LH needle.

② Slide the stitch to the other end of the CN and knit onto RH needle.

C2F (Cable 2 Front) with CN

① Work to stitch to be cabled. Slip next stitch onto a CN, hold at the front of the work, and knit the next stitch from the LH needle.

② Slide the stitch to the other end of the CN and knit onto RH needle.

Twisting stitches

When a cable-style pattern is prefixed with a "T" it means that the cable effect is achieved by using a mixture of knit and purl stitches. This technique is used for creating diamonds, lattice, and more complicated cable patterns. Like cables, the number of stitches in a twist can vary. Twists can be worked over a variety of regular stitches. All the cabling is worked on the RS of the work.

THREE-STITCH TWIST

A three-stitch twist cable consists of knitting two of the stitches and purling one stitch. The effect is of traveling lines of knit stitch.

T3B (Twist 3 Back) with CN

Here 2 stitches are moved to form a right diagonal against a background of rev st.st.

① (RS): Work to 1 stitch before the 2 knit stitches to be cabled. Slip next stitch onto CN and hold at back of work. Knit the next 2 stitches from LH needle.

② Now purl the stitch from the CN.

T3F (Twist 3 Front) with CN

Here 2 stitches are moved to form a left diagonal against a background of rev st.st.

① (RS): Work to the 2 knit stitches to be cabled and slip these 2 stitches onto a CN and hold at front of work. Purl next stitch from the LH needle.

② Knit the 2 stitches from CN.

TWO-STITCH TWIST

Two-stitch twists can be worked on the right- or wrong-side rows and with or without a CN. Twisting stitches without a CN takes practice, but it can speed up the knitting greatly. This technique is described on page 57.

T2B (Twist 2 Back) With CN

① Work to 1 stitch before the knit stitch to be cabled. Slip next stitch onto a CN and hold at back of work. Knit the next stitch from LH needle.

② Now purl the stitch from the CN.

T2F (Twist 2 Front) With CN

① Work to the knit stitch to be cabled and slip this stitch onto a CN and leave at the front of the work. Purl the next stitch from LH needle.

② Now knit the stitch from the CN.

Shaping techniques

The techniques used for shaping can make or break a finished piece. There are simple rules to follow for creating "fully fashioned" shaping. Combined with mattress stitch for sewing up, the finished piece should, with practice, look seamless.

INCREASING

There are a few methods for increasing stitches, but for forming extra stitches within a row there is none better than mattress stitch. It is best worked two or three stitches in from the edge of a piece to make a feature of the shaping (see Aran bag, page 90). Probably the neatest form of increasing stitches is the "Make 1" technique because it involves working between stitches instead of into a stitch, thus reducing bulk. The technique can be worked as a knit or a purl stitch as follows:

M1K (Make 1 stitch knitwise)

① *Insert the RH needle from front to back under the horizontal strand that lies between the last stitch knitted on the RH needle and the next stitch to be knitted on the LH needle.*

② *Lift the strand onto the LH needle and knit into the back of it. Knitting into the back of the stitch prevents a hole from forming and creates a flat, neat increase.*

M1P (Make 1 stitch purlwise)

① *Work as for M1K, but purl into back of stitch thus: Turn LH needle in a clockwise direction until it lies almost parallel with RH needle.*

② *Insert RH needle in a purlwise direction (from right to left) into M1 loop. Have the tip of the RH needle under that of the LH needle. Turn LH needle back and complete the purl stitch.*

DECREASING

Many knitters assume there is only one technique for decreasing a stitch at the beginning and end of a row—K2tog. This will decrease a stitch, but bear in mind that the stitch will lie in one direction—it will be angled to the right. For a fully fashioned look, use in conjunction with the K2togtbl, which angles the decrease to the left. For shaping the Aran bag (page 90), k2togtbl was used at the beginning of the decrease rows and k2tog at the end, allowing the stitches to lie in the direction of the shaping.

K2TOG (knit two stitches together)
Thus decreasing 1 stitch, which is angled to the right. The second stitch will lie on top of the first.

K2TOGTBL (knit two stitches together through back of loops)
Thus decreasing 1 stitch, which is angled to the left. The first stitch will lie on top of the second.

SKP (slip 1, knit 1, pass slipped stitch over)
As an alternative to K2togtbl, the decrease is angled to the left.

Insert RH needle into front of the next two stitches on LH needle and draw the loop through and drop both stitches off the LH needle.

Insert RH needle into the back loops of the next two stitches on LH needle and draw the loop through and drop both stitches off the LH needle.

Slip the next stitch onto RH needle, knit the following stitch and lift the slipped stitch over the second stitch to decrease.

SLIP STITCHES

Slip stitches are used in stitch patterns and decreasing. The stitch is simply passed from one needle to the other without working it, thus no new stitch is formed.

Sl.1 (Slip 1 stitch knitwise)
Insert RH needle into the next stitch on LH needle as if to knit.

Do not take the yarn around needle. Pass stitch to RH needle.

Sl.1p (Slip 1 stitch purlwise)
Slipping stitches purlwise allows the stitch to lie in the same direction as a knit stitch. Insert the RH needle into the next stitch as if to purl. Do not take yarn around needle and pass the stitch to the RH needle.

Rejoining yarn

There is nothing more infuriating than finding that the bead order is wrong or that the yarn runs out mid-project. A quick solution is to undo stitches to the beginning of the row, cut yarn, and reorder the beads before rejoining the yarn to continue. Joining in a new color is done in the same way. This process will entail some very neat darning of the resulting tail ends.

Leaving a 2 in tail end, wrap yarn around needle and hold the yarn and the tail end before completing the stitch. Drop the tail end and continue in pattern across the row.

Joining seams

Many knitters master the knitting techniques easily, but let themselves down when it comes to finishing. It is important to treat the seams as part of the overall design. Often the simplest pattern, made in good-quality yarn and beautifully finished, is the most professional-looking piece. The following two methods will produce just such results.

MATTRESS STITCH

The neatest, most professional seam, mattress stitch is worked on the RS of the work. This makes matching patterns and shaping much easier because it allows you to see where you are. Combining a mattress stitch seam with the increasing and decreasing techniques outlined in this section produces a fully fashioned shape. The shaping is worked a couple of stitches in from the edge to form a straight edge for sewing; the seam can be sewn either half a stitch or one stitch in. When sewing, it is easier to work from the cast-on edge vertically. Always use a round-ended knitters' darning needle to avoid splitting the yarn.

① *Using the tail end at the cast-on edge of the first side, thread onto needle. Take the needle under the cast-on edge of the second side to be joined and pull through until edges are drawn together and level.*

② *Now insert needle into first stitch on first side and out of the second stitch on same side, picking up the horizontal bar in the process. Draw yarn through. Rep for second side and gently pull yarn to draw both pieces together.*

③ *Now insert needle into second stitch on first side and out of the third stitch, again picking up the horizontal bar. Draw yarn through. Rep for second side. Continue to work in this way until the seam is finished. If sewn correctly, both sides of the knitting should be level at the top. If they are not, it usually means that a stitch has been missed on the shorter side.*

OVERSEW STITCH

Oversew stitch is ideal for sewing two cast-on edges together as it replicates the cast-on stitch. This seam has been used to sew the bottom edge of the Aran bag (page 90). Again, the seam is worked on the RS to make it easier to match the stitches.

*With WS together, insert the needle under the first cast-on stitches of both fabrics to be joined. Draw needle through from front to back. * Bringing needle and yarn to the front, insert the needle under the next pair of stitches and draw through to the back. Rep from * to end.*

Finishing off with findings

The way findings are attached to a piece should be considered very carefully as part of the overall design and finish of the project. The right choice of findings will greatly enhance a piece of jewelry giving it a really professional look.

ATTACHING JUMP RINGS WITH PLIERS

Jump rings should be attached carefully by opening and closing them laterally instead of pulling them apart, which will distort the shape.

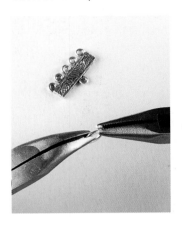

A couple of lightweight, flat-nosed pliers are best used for the job. Here, one of the pairs has an angled head.

ATTACHING CALOTTES

Think of a calotte as a tiny hinged box for hiding unsightly tail ends. A calotte will add a touch of professionalism to your work.

Knot the tail ends securely, trim the excess, and place into one half of the calotte. Line up the wire below the knot with the small nick in the bottom edge of the calotte. Carefully close, first pinching with your fingers, then squeezing with flat-nosed pliers to secure.

MAKING AN ADJUSTABLE CHOKER CLASP

Adjustable choker clasps can be bought in sets, but they are expensive and can be limited in size and finishes. However, they are simple to make as follows:

Attach a lobster clasp to the single hole of an end connector with a jump ring. To the single hole of a second end connector, attach a length of chain, approx 3¼ —4 in in length, using a larger jump ring.

Sewing on beads

If the bead design is particularly complicated, the beads can be sewn onto the finished knitted piece. For larger holed beads, knitting yarn can be used, but sewing thread and a fine beading needle is necessary for seed beads and bugle beads.

Join yarn to the back of the work with a couple of small stitches. Bring needle to the RS of the work and thread on a bead. Take needle back through to WS a bead width from start point, then bring to RS of work for the next bead.

Embroidering on knitted fabric

Knitting can be enhanced with simple embroidery stitches, as in traditional Swiss Tyrolean designs. Embroidery can be worked in knitting yarns or tapestry wools, or try embroidery silks for a luxurious look.

SATIN STITCH

LAZY DAISY STITCH

Join yarn to the back of the work with a couple of small stitches. Bring needle to the RS of the work and back through to WS to create a short stitch. Keeping the stitches close together, make more stitches in the same way to create a slightly raised surface.

① Join yarn to the back of the work with a couple of small stitches. Bring needle to the RS of the work and make a loop with the yarn. Insert needle back into start point and take up a stitch to form the length of the daisy petal.

② Holding the loop in place with thumb, draw through the needle and yarn. Secure loop in place by taking needle through to WS.

Abbreviations

CN	Cable needle	LH	Left hand	st(s)	Stitch(es)
col	Color	mm	Millimeters	st.st	Stockinette stitch
C2B	Cable (cross) 2 Back	M1K	Make one stitch knitwise	T2B	Twist 2 Back
C2F	Cable (cross) 2 Front	M1P	Make one stitch purlwise	T2F	Twist 2 Front
in	Inch	p	Purl	T3B	Twist 3 Back
k	Knit	p1B	Purl 1 bead	T3F	Twist 3 Front
kB1	Knit into back of stitch	rep	Repeat	WS	Wrong side
kfb	Knit into front and back of stitch	rem	Remaining	yfwd	Yarn forward
		RH	Right hand	ybk	Yarn back
k1B	Knit 1 bead	RS	Right side	yd	Yard
k2tog	Knit 2 together	skp	Slip 1, K1, pass slipped stitch over		
k2togtbl	Knit 2 together through back loops	sl.1	Slip one stitch		

THE PROJECTS

1 getting you started

These simple projects have been designed for those who are new to knitting and for those working with beads and wire for the first time. Quick to make, there is no reason why the most experienced knitter couldn't churn out these projects by the bucketful!

2 working with cotton yarns

If you haven't tried knitting with cotton yarns before, or if you don't like knitted cotton garments, then try these lovely jewelry projects. Basic yarns have been used throughout, which are available in a multitude of colors to suit every taste.

3 discs, sequins, and drops

This is where the real fun begins! Introducing different shapes and textures in the form of discs, sequins, and drops will produce amazing and very glamorous results. The simplest patterns come first in this section, so don't be scared to give them a go—you'll be surprised at what you can produce in an evening!

4 for the more experienced

Never tried Aran knitting? Your shaping techniques leave a lot to be desired? These projects offer you a good introduction to more complex patterns, but with the added advantage that they are on a small scale and are achievable with just a bit more skill and concentration.

Glass bead and leather cord wristband

The large crystal seed beads contrast beautifully with the deep bronze color of the fine leather cord to produce a simple but very striking wristband. Team with your favorite piece of cheesecloth and you have the perfect "hippy chick" look. For those who would prefer not to use real leather, there are excellent cotton substitutes on the market.

★ Captioned step-by-step pictures on page 38

★ HOT TIP
Adding four beads for every extra row knitted can lengthen the piece. The more ambitious knitter could attempt a choker.

★ SPECIAL INSTRUCTIONS
The leather has a certain amount of stretch, so pull it tight when winding to keep the stitches even. The loopy effect is created by winding the yarn twice around the needle for each stitch. The extra loop is then dropped on the following row.

The wristband

MATERIALS FOR WRISTBAND
• 5½ yd. leather cord, size 1 mm, col bronze
• 88 x transparent seed beads, size 5/0, col crystal
• Pair US 9 knitting needles

FINISHED SIZE
Length, excluding drawstring: 6¾ in.
Width: 2¾ in.

BEAD SET UP
Thread on 84 beads.

WRISTBAND
Leaving a 8½ in. tail end, using US 9 needles and cord, cast on 4 sts very loosely.
Row 1: Bring up one bead for each stitch and knit to end, winding yarn around needle twice for each stitch: (8 loops on needle).
Row 2: Bring up one bead for each stitch. Winding yarn around the needle twice and dropping one loop of each stitch from the previous row, knit to end. Rep row 2 until 21 rows have been completed and all beads have been worked.
Bind off very loosely.
Leaving a 10-in. tail end, cut cord and fasten off.

FINISHING
Weave one tail end to center of bound-off end and tie a knot to secure to center stitch. Rep for the other tail end.
Make drawstring fastening: Using one tail end, work two half-hitch knots close to end of knitting. Thread two beads onto one tail end and tie a knot at the end. Make a knot above the beads to secure them in place. Using the last two beads, rep for the other tail end.

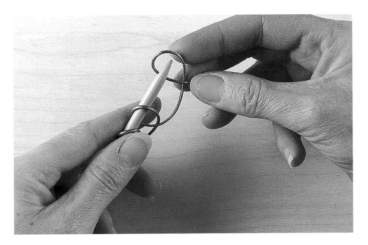

① *Casting on using the loop method.*

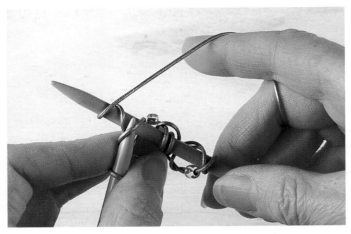

② *Knitting a stitch; winding the yarn twice around the needle.*

③ *Knitting a stitch; preparing to drop one of the loops.*

④ *Weaving a tail end to the center stitch.*

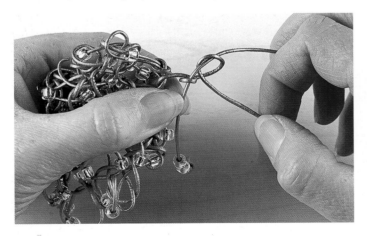

⑤ *Working the half hitch knots; second knot being made.*

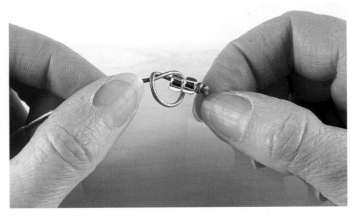

⑥ *Securing beads with a knot to decorate tail ends.*

Rings

These pretty rings can be attempted by a complete beginner and are very quick to knit. Threading on the 33 beads will probably take longer than the knitting. Experiment with using different colors; here the first pattern is mainly red with a central, slightly larger lilac bead, while the second pattern shows that a diagonal pattern will be achieved by alternating two bead colors.

★ Captioned step-by-step pictures on page 40

Red bead ring with lilac bead center

MATERIALS FOR RED BEAD RING WITH LILAC BEAD CENTER
- Small spool wire, size 0.20 mm (32 AWG), col light gold
- 32 x faceted, transparent glass beads, size 6 mm, col red AB
- 1 x faceted, transparent glass bead, size 8 mm, col lilac
- Pair US 0 knitting needles
- Sewing needle

FINISHED SIZE
Length: 2½ in.
Width: ¾ in.

BEAD SET UP
Thread on 16 red, 1 lilac, and 16 red beads.

RED RING
Leave a 2-in. tail end.
Using US 0 needles and wire, cast on 3 sts.

Row 1 (WS): (K1B) 3 times.
Row 2: Purl.
Rep rows 1 and 2 until all beads have been worked, ending row 1.
Bind off purlwise.
Leaving a 2-in. tail end, cut wire and fasten off.

FINISHING
Bend piece to form a circle. Thread one of the tail ends onto sewing needle and slip stitch to form a flat seam. Finish off both tail ends through the beads. Trim close to work.

▷

① *Threading beads onto the wire.*

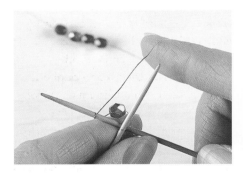

② *Casting on the third stitch; putting the stitch onto LH needle.*

③ *K1B; knitting a beaded stitch.*

④ *Joining the seam using a flat seam.*

Crystal and blue diagonal ring

MATERIALS FOR CRYSTAL AND BLUE DIAGONAL RING

- Small spool wire, size 0.20 mm (32 AWG), col silver plate
- 17 x faceted transparent glass beads, size 6 mm, col crystal AB
- 16 x faceted transparent glass beads, size 6 mm, col blue
- Pair US 0 knitting needles
- Sewing needle

FINISHED SIZE

Length: 2½ in.
Width: ¾ in.

BEAD SET UP

Thread 1 crystal, *1 blue, 1 crystal, rep from * until all beads are threaded onto wire.

CRYSTAL AND BLUE DIAGONAL RING

Leave a 2-in. tail end.
Using US 0 needles and 2 mm wire, cast on 3 sts.
Row 1 (WS): (K1B) 3 times.
Row 2: Purl.
Rep rows 1 and 2 until all beads have been worked, ending row 1.
Bind off purlwise.
Leaving a 2-in. tail, cut wire and fasten off.

FINISHING

Bend piece to form a circle. Thread one of the tail ends onto sewing needle and slip stitch to form a flat seam. Finish off both tail ends through the beads. Trim close to work.

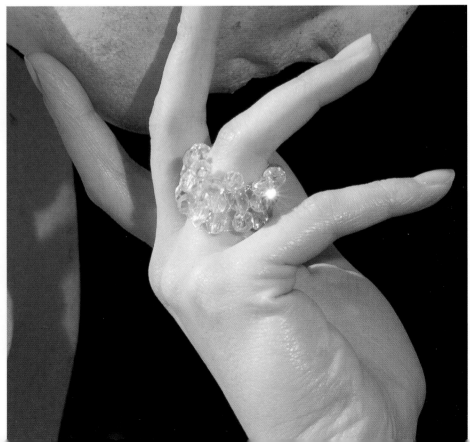

Bead-mix choker and wristband set

This set is perfect if you want the glamour and sparkle of multi-beaded pieces, but without the weight of glass. There are some interesting plastic beads available in multi packs and these designs feature Old World–style beads, which can add a touch of Mayan design to the pieces. Once the beads have been threaded, these pieces can be knitted in an evening and can easily be attempted by a beginner.

✱ Captioned step-by-step pictures on pages 42–43

✱ Hot Tip
Divide the beads into dishes according to size and when threading aim for an even spread of all sizes and textures.

✱ Special Instructions
The mixed beads are worked singly and the seed beads are worked in pairs throughout.

The Choker

MATERIALS FOR CHOKER
- Small spool wire, size 0.20 mm (32 AWG), col black
- 90 x mixed plastic beads, col purple shades, and Old World containing the following:
- Faceted beads, sizes 12 mm, 10 mm, 6 mm

- Faceted bicones, sizes 13 x 6 mm and 10 x 7 mm
- Smooth round plastic beads, size 6 mm
- Pony beads, heart and flower shapes
- Old World-style gold plastic beads
- 538 x silver-lined seed beads, size 10/0, col silver
- 2 silver end connectors (5 holes on one side and 1 hole on the other), 25 mm wide
- 1 medium silver lobster clasp
- 6¾ in. length of silver chain
- 5 mm silver jump ring
- 9 mm silver jump ring
- Pair US 9 knitting needles
- Sewing needle

FINISHED SIZE
Length, excluding findings: 11 in.
Width: 1¾ in.

BEAD SET UP
Thread on * 1 bead, 2 seed, 1 bead, 2 seed, 1 bead, 12 seed, 1 bead, 2 seed, 1 bead, 12 seed, rep from * until all 90 mixed beads have been threaded onto wire, ending last rep with 10 seeds.

CHOKER
Leave a 4¾ in. tail end.
Using US 9 needles and wire, bringing up 2 seeds for each st, cast on 5 sts.
NB: the slip knot is not beaded.
Now work in garter stitch throughout (K1B), bringing up the beads as set for each st.
Cont in garter stitch until all the beads have been knitted.
Bind off loosely. Leaving a 4-in tail end, cut wire and fasten off.

FINISHING
Join the lobster clasp to one of the end connectors with the 5 mm jump ring. Thread one of the tail ends onto sewing needle and sew the connector holes to the end of the choker. Join the other connector to the length of chain with the 9 mm jump ring and sew to the other end of the choker. Finish off tail ends and trim close to work. ▷

❶ *Sorting beads before threading onto the wire.*

❷ *Casting on with seed beads; putting the stitch onto LH needle.*

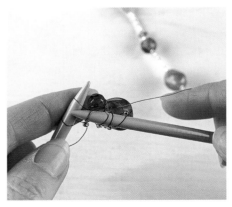

❸ *K1B; wrapping wire with a bead in place.*

④ K1B; wrapping wire with two seed beads in place.

⑤ Sewing on an end connector with a lobster clasp attached.

⑥ Sewing on a clasp for the wristband using a tail end.

The wristband

MATERIALS FOR WRISTBAND

- Small spool wire, size 0.20 mm (32 ANG), col black
- 45 x mixed plastic beads as choker, col black mix
- 268 x silver-lined seed beads, size 10/0, col silver
- Toggle clasp, size 16 mm clasp and 22 mm toggle, col pewter
- Pair US 9 knitting needles
- Sewing needle

FINISHED SIZE

Length, including findings: 7 in.
Width: 1¾ in.

BEAD SET UP

Thread on * 1 bead, 2 seed, 1 bead, 2 seed, 1 bead, 12 seed, 1 bead, 2 seed, 1 bead, 12 seed, rep from * until all 45 mixed beads have been threaded onto wire, ending last rep with 10 seeds.

WRISTBAND

Leave a 4 in tail end.
Using US 9 needles and wire, bringing up 2 seeds for each st, cast on 5 sts.
NB: the slip knot is not beaded.
Now work in garter stitch throughout, bringing up the beads as set for each st.
Cont in garter stitch until all the beads have been knitted.
Bind off loosely. Leaving a 4 in. tail end, cut wire, and fasten off.

FINISHING

Weave tail end through bound-off end of knitting to center. Thread tail end onto sewing needle and, keeping stitches loose, stitch through connector hole of toggle and the knitting a few times to secure. Rep for cast-on end, sewing to the connector hole of the clasp. Wind tail ends around shanks to finish off. Trim wire close to work.

Crystal bicone and seed bead wristband

The seed beads used in this project are color-lined in purple, which perfectly complements the colors produced by the iridescent finish of the crystal bicones. This results in an effect of jagged crystalline, almost icicle formations.

✴ Captioned step-by-step pictures on page 46

✴ SPECIAL INSTRUCTIONS

The bicones are worked singly and the seed beads are worked in pairs throughout.

Bringing up a bead after a slip stitch (sl.1) allows the bead to lie on the right side of a knit row. Hold the bead at the front of the work with your thumb to avoid the bead moving to the wrong side of the work when you take the yarn back for the knit stitch.

The wristband

MATERIALS

- Small spool wire, size 0.20 mm (32 AWG), col silver plated
- 75 x transparent glass faceted bicones, size 12 x 7 mm, col crystal AB
- 150 x color-lined transparent seed beads, size 7/0, col lined in purple
- 2 silver magnetic clasps, size 15mm
- Pair US 7 knitting needles
- Sewing needle

FINISHED SIZE:

Length, excluding findings: 6 in.
Width: 2½ in.

BEAD SET UP

Thread on * 2 seed beads,1 bicone, rep from * until all beads have been threaded onto wire.

WRISTBAND

Leave a 6¼ in. tail end.
Using US 7 needles and wire cast on 11 sts.

Row 1: K1, yfwd, sl.1, bring up bicone, ybk, k1, * yfwd, sl.1, bring up seeds, ybk, k1, yfwd, sl.1, bring up bicone, ybk, k1, rep from * to end.
Row 2: K1, p9, k1.
Row 3: K1, yfwd, sl.1, bring up seeds, ybk, k1, * yfwd, sl.1, bring up bicone, ybk, k1, yfwd, sl.1, bring up seeds, ybk, k1, rep from * to end.
Row 4: K1, p9, k1.
Rep last 4 rows until 56 rows have been completed.
Work rows 1 to 3 once more.
Bind off.
Leaving a 6¼ in. tail end, cut wire and fasten off.

FINISHING

Thread one of the tail ends onto sewing needle and spacing them evenly, sew the two magnetic clasps onto one end of the wristband. Rep for the other end of the wristband. Finish off tail ends and trim close to work.

1 *Beads threaded onto the wire.*

2 *Casting on; putting the 11th stitch onto LH needle.*

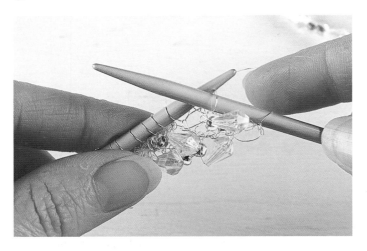

3 *Sl.1 with bicone; taking ybk, bicone is in place ready for knitting next stitch.*

4 *Sl.1 with seed beads; taking ybk, seed beads are in place ready for knitting next stitch.*

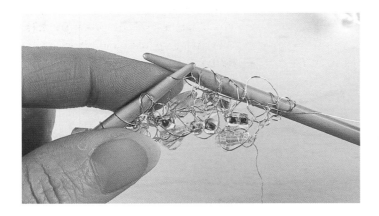

5 *Purling on the WS rows; preparing to take off stitch.*

6 *Sewing one half of the magnetic clasp using a tail end.*

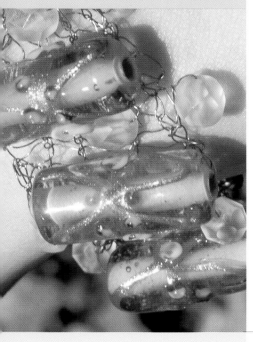

Bracelet with Venetian-style beads

The style of glass bead used here, known as Fiorato, is created using melted glass to paint the flowers and decorations. Because the beads are handmade, their sizes and shapes will vary. The traditional methods used by the Murano glass bead-makers are very closely guarded secrets passed down through the generations. Venetian beads give instant added value to any piece of jewelry.

✳ Captioned step-by-step pictures on page 48

✳ SPECIAL INSTRUCTIONS

KB1: The WS rows worked after the Venetian bead rows instruct the knitter to "knit into back of stitch". Knitting into the back of a stitch will tighten the stitch in the row below and here it will hold the Venetian bead in place.

The bracelet

MATERIALS

• Small spool wire, size 0.20 mm (32 AWG), col gun bronze
• 8 x Venetian-style glass beads, size 20 mm, col olive green
• 33 x matte glass faceted beads, size 6 mm, col pink AB
• Toggle clasp, size 10 mm clasp and 20 mm toggle, col bronze
• Pair US 3 knitting needles
• Sewing needle

FINISHED SIZE

Length, excluding findings: 6 in.
Width: 1 in.

BEAD SET UP

Thread on 6 glass faceted beads, 1 Venetian bead, * 3 glass beads, 1 Venetian, rep from * until 8 Venetian beads have been threaded, ending with 6 glass faceted beads.

BRACELET

Leave a 3¼ in. tail end.
Using US 3 needles and wire, cast on 5 sts.
Row 1 (RS): K1B, k1, p1B, k1, k1B.
Row 2: Purl.
Row 3: Knit.
Row 4: Purl.
Rep rows 1 to 4 once more.
Row 9: K1, yfwd, sl.3, bring up a bead, ybk, k1.
Row 10: KB1, p3, kB1.
Row 11: Knit.

Row 12: Purl.
Row 13: K1B, k1, p1B, k1, k1B.
Row 14: Purl.
Row 15: Knit.
Row 16: Purl.
Rep rows 9 to 16 until 8 Venetian beads have been worked, ending with row 16.
Then work row 13 again.
Bind off purlwise.
Leaving a 3¼ in. tail end, cut wire and fasten off.

FINISHING

Thread one tail end onto sewing needle. Weave to center of bound-off edge and use to sew on a clasp. Rep for the cast-on end, using the tail to sew on toggle. Darn in tail ends and trim close to work.

▷

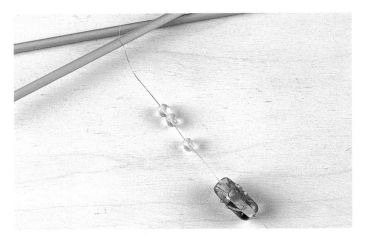

1 *Beads threaded onto the wire.*

2 *K1B; wrapping wire knitwise with a faceted bead in place.*

3 *P1B; wrapping wire purlwise with a faceted bead in place.*

4 *Sl.3; taking ybk, Venetian bead is in place ready for knitting next stitch.*

5 *KB1; inserting needle into back of stitch to knit a tighter stitch.*

6 *Sewing on clasp using a tail end.*

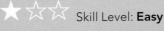

Skill Level: **Easy**

Bands with wooden beads

A very simple knitting pattern has been used effectively here to create bands of varying widths for the neck, wrist, and ankle. Variations can be made by changing the bead colors and the widths of the bands to suit every taste. These are lovely quick-to-make gifts for your friends and family.

★ Captioned step-by-step pictures on page 52

★ HOT TIP

Use a small piece of grid paper and some colored pencils to chart your own bead patterns. When the design is finished, thread the beads by starting at the top right corner of the chart and work from right to left across the rows.

The choker

MATERIALS FOR CHOKER
- 1 x 1¾ oz. ball 4-ply cotton yarn, col natural
- 45 x wooden beads, size 8 mm, col pink
- 45 x wooden beads, size 8 mm, col natural
- 2 silver end connectors (5 holes on one side and 1 hole on the other), 20 mm wide
- 1 medium silver lobster clasp
- 5 mm silver jump ring
- 9 mm silver jump ring
- 10 cm silver chain
- Pair US 3 knitting needles
- Sewing needle

FINISHED SIZE:
Length, excluding findings: 11 in.
Width: ¾ in.

BEAD SET UP
Thread on * 1 natural, 1 pink, rep from * until 90 beads have been threaded onto the cotton yarn.

CHOKER
Leave a 4-in. tail end.
Using US 3 needles and yarn, cast on 60 sts.
Row 1 (WS): * K1B, k1, rep from * to end.
Row 2: Knit.
Row 3: * K1, k1B, rep from * to end.
Row 4: Knit.
Row 5: As row 1.
Bind off.
Leaving a 4-in. tail end, cut yarn and fasten off.

FINISHING
Join the lobster clasp to one of the end connectors with the 9 mm jump ring. Splitting the yarn, thread one of the tail ends onto a sewing needle and sew the connector holes to the end of the choker. Join the other connector to the length of chain with the 5 mm jump ring and sew to the other end of the choker. Finish off tail ends and trim close to work.

① *Charting a design on grid paper.*

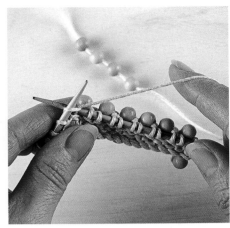

② *K1B; wrapping yarn with a wooden bead in place.*

③ *K1; bringing loop through to finish a stitch.*

④ *Sewing on an end connector by splitting the yarn tail end.*

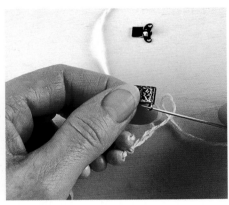

⑤ *Sewing on one half of a box clasp by splitting the yarn tail end.*

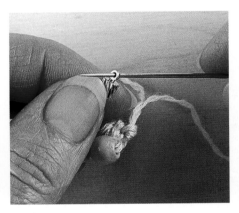

⑥ *Sewing on a magnetic clasp by splitting the yarn tail end.*

The wristband

MATERIALS FOR WRISTBAND

- 1 x 1¾ oz. ball 4-ply cotton yarn, col natural
- 18 x wooden beads, size 8 mm, col brown
- 16 x wooden beads, size 8 mm, col green
- 1 silver filigree box clasp
- Pair US 3 knitting needles
- Sewing needle

FINISHED SIZE

Length, including findings: 6¼ in.
Width: ⅝ in.

BEAD SET UP

Thread on (* 1 brown, 1 green, rep from * until 17 beads have been threaded) twice: 34 beads threaded onto yarn.

WRISTBAND

Leave a 4-in. tail end.
Using US 3 needles and yarn, cast on 33 sts.

Row 1 (WS): K1B, * k1, k1B, rep. from * to end.
Row 2: Knit.
Row 3: As row 1.
Bind off.
Leaving a 4-in. tail end, cut yarn and fasten off.

FINISHING

Splitting the yarn, thread one of the tail ends onto sewing needle and use to sew one half of the box clasp to end of wristband. Rep for other end.

The anklet

MATERIALS FOR ANKLET

- 1 x 3 ¼ oz. ball 4-ply yarn, col natural
- 10 x wooden beads, size 8 mm, col yellow
- 6 x wooden beads, size 8 mm, col pink
- 3 x wooden beads, size 8 mm, col green
- 1 gold magnetic clasp, size 15 mm
- Pair US 3 knitting needles
- Sewing needle

FINISHED SIZE:
Length, including findings: 6¾ in.
Width: ½ in.

BEAD SET UP

1 yellow, 1 pink, * 1 yellow, 1 pink, 1 yellow, 1 green, rep from * twice more, (1 yellow, 1 pink) twice, 1 yellow: 19 beads threaded onto yarn.

ANKLET

Leave a 4-in. tail end.
Using US 3 needles and yarn, cast on 37 sts.

Row 1 (WS): K1B, * k1, k1B, rep. from * to end.
Bind off.
Leaving a 4-in. tail end, cut yarn and fasten off

FINISHING

Splitting the yarn, thread one of the tail end strands onto a needle, and use to sew one half of the magnetic clasp to the center of one end of the anklet. Rep for the other end, sewing the other half of the clasp. Darn off remaining strands. Trim close.

Seed bead thread bracelets

These pretty bracelets are surprisingly simple to make. Knitted in stockinette stitch, using a fine mercerized crochet thread, the beads are worked using a slip stitch, which holds the bead to the knit side of the pattern. The tube effect is created because the stockinette-stitch edges naturally form a roll. Finish off each end with a large glass bead; silver antique-style end caps, beads, and findings give an exotic touch.

✳ Captioned step-by-step pictures on page 56

✳ HOT TIP
Hold the bead at the front of the work with your thumb to avoid the bead moving to the wrong side of the work when you take the yarn back for the knit stitch.

✳ SPECIAL INSTRUCTIONS
Bringing up a bead after a slip stitch (sl.1) allows the bead to lie on the right side of a knit row.

The single color bracelet

MATERIALS FOR SINGLE COLOR BRACELET
• 1 x 1¾ oz. ball Coats AIDA 5 100% thread, col cream
• 147 x color-lined transparent seed beads, size 7/0, col pink

• 2 x crackle-effect glass beads, size 8 mm, col cerise
• 2 silver metal beads, size 8 mm
• 2 silver conical end caps, size 20 mm length
• Toggle clasp, size 12 mm clasp and 15 mm toggle, col silver
• Pair US 0 knitting needles
• Sewing needle

FINISHED SIZE
Length, including findings: 8¼ in.
Width, rolled: ¾ in.

BEAD SET UP
Thread on 147 pink seed beads.

BRACELET
Leave a 6-in. tail end.
Using US 0 needles and thread, cast on 11 sts.
Work 6 rows st.st.
Now work bead pattern:
Row 1 (RS): K3, * yfwd, sl.1, bring up a bead, ybk, k1, rep from * to last 2 sts, k2.
Row 2: Purl.

Row 3: K2, * yfwd, sl.1, bring up a bead, ybk, k1, rep from * to last st, k1.
Row 4: Purl.
Rep rows 1 to 4 until all beads have been worked: (21 repeats).
Work 6 rows st.st.
Bind off.
Leaving a 6-in. tail end, cut thread and fasten off.

FINISHING
Allow the piece to roll into a tube. Thread one tail end onto sewing needle and work 2 oversew sts to secure the tube. Thread the tail through an end cap, one of the 8 mm silver beads, an 8 mm glass bead, and the connector hole of the clasp. Now thread back through all the beads and the end cap. Pull so all the beads lie tightly together. Rep once more after taking up a stitch from the end of the knitting. Darn off the remaining tail end.
Trim thread close to work.
Rep for the other end, joining the connector hole of the toggle.

① Sl.1 with a seed bead; taking ybk, seed bead is in place for knitting next st.

② WS row; purling stitches. The stockinette stitch curls to form a tube.

③ Over sewing tail end to secure the end of the tube.

④ Threading a tail end through end cap, silver and glass beads, and clasp.

⑤ Pulling the tail end to tighten the findings.

⑥ Darning off remaining tail end into back of work.

The diagonal-pattern bracelet

MATERIALS FOR DIAGONAL-PATTERN BRACELET

- 1 x 1¾ oz. ball Coats AIDA 5 100% cotton, col cream
- 74 x silver-lined seed beads, size 7/0, col ice blue
- 73 x silver-lined seed beads, size 7/0, col bronze
- 2 x crackle-effect glass beads, size 8 mm, col yellow
- 2 silver metal beads, size 8 mm
- 2 silver conical end caps, size 20 mm length
- 1 Toggle clasp, size 12 mm clasp and 15 mm toggle, col silver
- Pair US 0 knitting needles
- Sewing needle

FINISHED SIZE

Length, including findings: 8¼ in.
Width, rolled: ¾ in.

BEAD SET UP

Thread on 1 blue, * 1 bronze, 1 blue, rep from * until 147 seed beads have been threaded.

DIAGONAL-PATTERN BRACELET

Leave a 6-in. tail end.
Using US 0 needles and thread, cast on 11 sts.
Work 6 rows st.st.
Now work bead pattern:
Row 1 (RS): K3, * yfwd, sl.1, bring up a bead, ybk, k1, rep from * to last 2 sts, k2.
Row 2: Purl.
Row 3: K2, * yfwd, sl.1, bring up a bead, ybk, k1, rep from * to last st, k1.

Row 4: Purl.
Rep rows 1 to 4 until all beads have been worked: (21 repeats).
Work 6 rows st.st.
Bind off.
Leaving a 6-in. tail end, cut thread and fasten off. Allow piece to roll into a tube.

FINISHING

Thread one tail end onto sewing needle and work 2 oversew sts to secure the tube. Thread the tail through an end cap, an 8 mm silver bead, an 8 mm glass bead, and the connector hole of the clasp. Thread back through all the beads and the end cap. Pull so all the beads lie tight together. Rep after taking up a stitch from the end of the knitting. Darn off the tail end. Trim thread close to work. Rep for other end, joining the toggle.

Embroidered wristband and hair band

Inspired by traditional Tyrolean embroidered knitwear, these unusual pieces are made in cotton DK yarn, which is available in a multitude of colors. The beads are added during the knitting process and the embroidery is worked afterward. Simple embroidery stitches combine with the beads to create flowers and leaves. Budget allowing, substitute the DK cotton yarn with luxury yarns, such as silk or cashmere.

★ Captioned step-by-step pictures on pages 58–59

★ HOT TIP

Check and double check the bead set up before you start to avoid having to break the yarn to reorder beads.

★ SPECIAL INSTRUCTIONS

T2B: Slip next stitch onto CN and hold at back of work, knit next stitch from LH needle, then purl stitch from CN.
Or without a CN: Knit into front of second stitch on needle then purl first stitch, slipping both stitches off needle at the same time.
T2F: Slip next stitch onto CN and hold at front of work, purl next stitch from LH needle, then knit stitch from CN.
Or without a CN: Purl into the back of second stitch on needle, then knit first stitch, slipping both stitches off needle at the same time.
C2B: Slip next stitch onto CN and hold at back of work, knit next stitch from LH needle, then knit stitch from CN.

Or without a CN: Knit into front of second stitch on needle, then knit first stitch slipping both stitches off needle at the same time.
C2F: Slip next stitch onto CN and hold at front of work, knit next stitch from LH needle, then knit stitch from CN.
Or without a CN: Knit into the back of second stitch on needle then knit first stitch, slipping both stitches off needle at the same time.

The wristband

MATERIALS FOR WRISTBAND

- 1 x 1¾ oz. ball DK cotton yarn, col beige
- 37 x opaque seed beads, size 7/0, col orange
- 38 x opaque beads, size 7/0, col yellow
- Embroidery threads: pink, purple, green, and turquoise
- Pair US 0 knitting needles
- Cable needle
- B/1 crochet hook
- Knitter's needle

FINISHED SIZE

Length, excluding tie ends: 6¼ in.
Width: 2 in.

BEAD SET UP

Thread on 5 orange, 6 yellow, 1 orange, 5 yellow, 1 orange, * 1 yellow, 7 orange, 1 yellow, 1 orange, 5 yellow, 1 orange *, 5 yellow, 1 orange, rep from * to * once, 6 yellow, 5 orange: 67 beads threaded onto yarn.

▷

① *T2B; holding stitch to back of the work and preparing to knit next stitch.*

② *T2B; purling stitch from CN.*

③ *T2F; holding stitch at front of the work and preparing to purl next stitch.*

④ *T2F; knitting stitch from CN.*

⑤ *P1B; bringing up a bead and preparing to purl.*

⑥ *C2F; holding stitch to front and preparing to knit next stitch.*

WRISTBAND

Leave a 20-in. tail end.
Using US 0 needles and yarn, cast on 11 sts.
Row 1 (RS): K1, * p1B, k1, rep from * to end: (5 beads).
Row 2: K1, * p1, k1, rep from * to end. Rep row 2 twice more.
Row 5: K1, p1, k1, T2B, p1B, T2F, k1, p1, k1.
Row 6: (K1, p1) twice, k3, (p1, k1) twice.
Row 7: K1, p1, T2B, p1B, p1, p1B, T2F, p1, k1.
Row 8: K1, p2, k5, p2, k1.

Row 9: K1, T2B, p1B, p3, p1B, T2F, k1.
Row 10: K1, p1, k7, p1, k1.
Row 11: K2, p1B, (p2, p1B) twice, k2.
Row 12: As row 10.
Row 13: K1, T2F, p1B, p3, p1B, T2B, k1.
Row 14: As row 8.
Row 15: K1, p1, C2F, p1B, p1, p1B, C2B, p1, k1.
Row 16: As row 6.
Row 17: K1, p1B, k1, T2F, p1B, T2B, k1, p1B, k1.
Row 18: K1, p1, (k1, p2) twice, k1, p1, k1.
Row 19: K1, * p1B, k1, rep from * to end.
Row 20: As row 18.

Row 21: K1, p1B, k1, T2B, p1B, T2F, k1, p1B, k1.
Rep rows 6 to 21 once and then rows 6 to 16 once.
Next row: K1, p1, k1, T2F, p1B, T2B, k1, p1, k1.
Next row: As row 18.
Rep row 2 twice.
Next row: As row 1.
Bind off purlwise.
Leave a 20-in. tail end, cut yarn and fasten off.

7 *C2F; knitting next stitch from CN.*

8 *C2B; holding stitch at back, preparing to knit next stitch.*

9 *C2B; knitting stitch from CN.*

10 *Satin stitch embroidery; needle inserted to make stitch.*

11 *Lazy daisy stitch; loop formed and taking up a stitch.*

12 *Oversew; needle inserted from R to L through one loop of a twist stitch.*

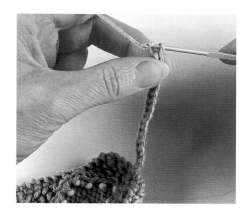  

13 *Crocheting chain; yarn over hook preparing to draw through a loop.*

14 *Threading on beads using a fine sewing thread.*

15 *Corners folded in to form a point. Elastic inserted and sewing to secure.* ▷

EMBROIDERY

Embroider the wristband using the chart, right, as a guide.

FINISHING

Using a knitter's needle, weave a tail end to center of the bound-off edge, ending with yarn on the WS of work. With RS of work facing, insert crochet hook from front to back and pull through a loop. Make a crochet chain of approximately 3 in. Pull through last loop. Thread 2 orange, 1 yellow, and 1 orange seed bead onto rem tail end. Knot the tail end to secure beads and trim.

Rep for the cast-on end.

KEY TO CHART

 Beads knitted into pattern

 Satin stitch embroidery— pink and purple

Lazy daisy stitch embroidery—green

Oversew embroidery— turquoise or red

 Beads knitted into pattern (hair band only)

The hair band

MATERIALS FOR HAIR BAND

- 1 x 1¾ oz. ball DK cotton yarn, col light blue
- 108 x opaque seed beads, size 7/0, col blue
- 52 x opaque seed beads, size 7/0, col red
- 35 x opaque seed beads, size 7/0, col yellow
- Embroidery threads: pink, purple, green, and red
- 4-in. length of ½ in. wide elastic
- Pair US 0 knitting needles
- Cable needle
- Sewing needle
- Knitter's needle

FINISHED SIZE

Length, excluding elastic: 17 in.
Width: 2 in.

BEAD SET UP

Thread on 1 yellow, * 4 blue, 1 red, 2 blue, 1 red, 1 yellow, 1 red, 2 blue, 1 red, 4 blue, 1 yellow, * 1 red, 1 yellow, 1 red, 1 yellow **. Rep from * to ** 7 times more, then from * to * once: 195 beads threaded onto yarn.

HAIR BAND

Leave a 8-in. tail end.
Using US 0 needles and yarn, cast on 11 sts.
Rows 1 and 2: K1, * p1, k1, rep from * to end.
Row 3: K1, (p1, k1) twice, p1B, (k1, p1) twice, k1.
Row 4: As row 1.
Row 5: K1, p1, k1, T2B, p1B, T2F, k1, p1, k1.
Row 6: (K1, p1) twice, k3, (p1, k1) twice.
Row 7: K1, p1, T2B, p1B, p1, p1B, T2F,

p1, k1.
Row 8: K1, p2, k5, p2, k1.
Row 9: K1, T2B, (p1B, p1) twice, p1B, T2F, k1.
Row 10: K1, p1, k7, p1, k1.
Row 11: K2, p1B, p1, (p1B) three times, p1, p1B, k2.
Row 12: As row 10.
Row 13: K1, T2F, (p1B, p1) twice, p1B, T2B, k1.
Row 14: As row 8.
Row 15: K1, p1, C2F, p1B, p1, p1B, C2B, p1, k1.
Row 16: As row 6.
Row 17: K1, p1, k1, T2F, p1B, T2B, k1, p1, k1.
Row 18: K1, p1, (k1, p2) twice, k1, p1, k1.
Row 19: K1, * p1B, k1, rep from * to end.

Row 20: As row 18.
Rep rows 5 to 20 seven times more.
Then rep rows 5 to 18 once.
Next row: As row 3.
Work 3 rows as row 1.
Bind off purlwise.
Cut yarn and fasten off.

EMBROIDERY

Embroider the hair band using the chart on the previous page as a guide.

FINISHING

Fold in corners to form a point at one end of the knitted band and insert one end of the elastic under the point. Sew in place and repeat for other end. Darn off tail ends.

Sequin and sparkle bracelet and earring set

This pretty bracelet and earring set is extremely quick and easy to make. All you need to master is casting on and binding off, and voila! These sequins and beads are available in numerous colors and finishes, so try experimenting with unusual contrasting colors or producing several sets, each in a different color, to create gifts to suit all tastes.

✱ Captioned step-by-step pictures on page 64–65

✱ HOT TIP
Make the earring first to practice keeping the cast-on and bound-off sts at the same tension.

✱ SPECIAL INSTRUCTIONS
The seed beads and sequins are knitted in the same stitch and the faceted beads are worked singly. In the bound-off row, the faceted beads will be knitted over the seed beads and sequins stitches of the cast-on row below.

The bracelet

MATERIALS FOR BRACELET
- Small spool wire, size 0.20 mm (32 AWG), col gun bronze
- 56 x sequins, size 6 mm, col lime green
- 29 x faceted transparent glass beads, size 6 mm, col lilac
- 112 x color-lined transparent seed beads, size 10/0, col pink fluorescent
- 1 gold magnetic clasp, size 15mm
- Pair US 7 knitting needles
- Sewing needle

FINISHED SIZE
Length, including findings: 21 cm
Width: 1 cm

BEAD SET UP
Thread on * 1 faceted bead, 2 seed beads, 2 sequins, 2 seed beads, rep from * 27 times more, 1 faceted bead.

BRACELET
Leave a 4-in. tail end.
Using US 7 needles and wire and bringing up beads as set for each stitch, cast on 29 sts.
NB: the slip knot is not beaded.
Bringing up beads as set for each stitch, bind off 29 sts.
Leaving a 4-in. tail end, cut wire and fasten off.

FINISHING
Thread tail ends onto sewing needle and use to sew one half of the magnetic clasp. Sew a few stitches to secure. Join a small length of wire to sew the other side of the magnetic clasp to the other end of the bracelet and sew securely. Darn in tail ends and trim close to work.

❶ Beads threaded onto wire to show sequence.

❷ Casting on a faceted bead; putting the stitch onto LH needle.

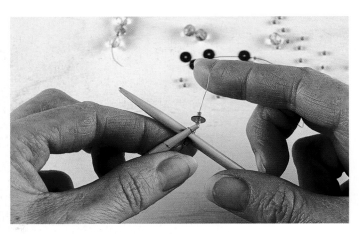

❸ Casting on seed beads and sequins; the seed beads and sequins are brought up as a set before wrapping the wire.

❹ Binding off with beads; bringing up the beads and sequins as set, lifting first stitch over second.

❺ Sewing on a magnetic clasp using a tail end.

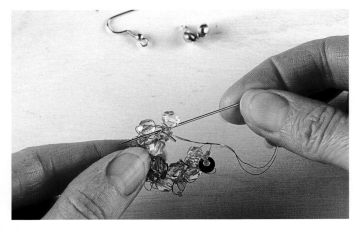

❻ Finishing the earring; sewing the two ends together.

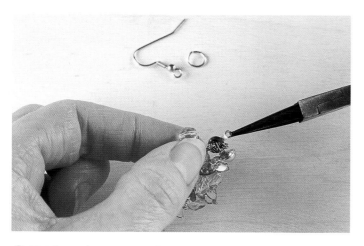

7 *Finishing the earring; placing the knotted tail ends into the calotte before closing.*

8 *Finishing the earring; joining the earring wire to the calotte with a jump ring.*

The earrings

MATERIALS FOR TWO EARRINGS

- Small spool wire, size 0.20 mm (32 AWG), col gun bronze
- 32 x sequins, size 6 mm, col lime green
- 18 x faceted transparent glass beads, size 6 mm, col lilac
- 64 x color-lined seed beads, size 10/0, col pink fluorescent
- 2 gold fish-hook earring wires
- 2 gold calottes
- 2 x 5 mm gold jump rings
- Pair US 7 knitting needles
- Sewing needle

FINISHED SIZE:

Length, to bend of fish hook: 2¼ in.
Width: 1 in.

BEAD SET UP

Thread on * 1 faceted bead, 2 seed, 2 sequins, 2 seed, rep from * 7 times more, 1 faceted bead.

EARRING (MAKE TWO)

Leave a 4-in. tail end.
Using US 7 needles and wire and bringing up beads as set for each stitch, cast on 9 sts.
NB: the slip knot is not beaded.
Bringing up beads as set for each stitch, bind off 9 sts.
Leaving a 4-in. tail end, cut wire and fasten off.

FINISHING

Twist together tail ends and thread onto sewing needle. Join to last stitch of piece to form a loop and make a few stitches to secure.
Make a knot with the rem tail ends and place in calotte. Gently squeeze calotte to close.
Join fish-hook earring wire to the calotte with a 5 mm jump ring.

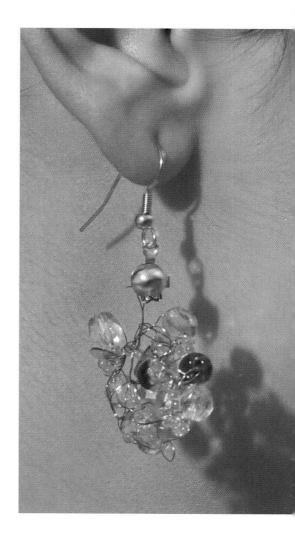

Silver disc necklace and earring set

Pretty glass faceted beads and sparkly silver seed beads are layered with shiny discs to create dramatic effect. This exquisite necklace and earring set looks impressive, but is surprisingly easy to make because there are only three stitches to work for each row. A very satisfying project for beginners and experienced knitters alike.

✱ Captioned step-by-step pictures on page 68

✱ SPECIAL INSTRUCTIONS
The faceted beads are worked singly and the discs and seed beads are worked in pairs throughout.

The necklace

MATERIALS FOR NECKLACE
- Small spool wire, size 0.20 mm (32 AWG), col silver plated
- 76 x discs, size 15 mm, col silver
- 37 x glass faceted beads, size 6 mm, col blue AB
- 156 x seed beads, size 10/0, col silver
- 1 silver lobster clasp
- 2 silver end connectors (3 holes on one side and 1 hole on the other), width 12 mm
- 2 silver 9 mm jump rings
- 1 silver 5 mm jump ring

- 12-in. length silver chain
- Pair US 3 knitting needles
- Sewing needle

FINISHED SIZE
Length, excluding findings: 6¾ in.
Width: ¾ in.

BEAD SET UP
Thread onto wire 6 seed, 2 discs, 1 bead, 2 discs, 6 seed, * 1 bead, 2 discs, 1 bead, 6 seed, 2 discs, 1 bead, 2 discs, 6 seed, rep from * 11 times more.

NECKLACE
Leave a 4-in. tail end.
Using US 3 needles and wire, cast on 3 sts.
Row 1 (RS): P1B every st to end: (6 seed).
Row 2: K1B every st to end: (2 discs, 1 bead, 2 discs).
Row 3: P1B every st to end: (6 seed).

Row 4: K1B every st to end: (1 bead, 2 discs, 1 bead).
Rep rows 1 to 4 another 11 times, then rep rows 1 to 3.
Do not bind off. Leaving a 4-in. tail end, cut wire.

FINISHING
Thread up last tail end onto sewing needle and use to sew each st to an end connector hole. Rep for the other end. Finish off tail ends. Divide the chain into two lengths; 8 in. and 4 in. Using the 5 mm jump ring, attach the lobster clasp to the shorter length of chain then attach the chain to the end connector using one of the 9 mm jump rings. Now join the longer length of chain to the other end connector using the rem 9 mm jump ring.

① *K1B; wrapping wire knitwise with discs in place.*

④ *Sewing stitches onto end connector using tail end.*

② *K1B; wrapping wire knitwise with faceted bead in place.*

⑤ *Finishing necklace; opening a jump ring to attach the chain to the end connector.*

③ *P1B; preparing to complete purl stitch with seed beads in place.*

⑥ *Finishing earring; joining the earring wire to the end connector.*

The earrings

MATERIALS FOR TWO EARRINGS

- Small spool wire, size 0.20 mm (32 AWG), col silver plated
- 36 x discs, size 15 mm, col silver
- 18 x glass faceted beads, size 6 mm, col blue AB
- 72 x seed beads, size 10/0, col silver
- 2 silver fish-hook earring wires
- 2 silver end connectors (3 holes on one side and 1 hole on the other), width 12 mm
- Pair US 3 knitting needles
- Sewing needle

FINISHED SIZE
Length, to bend in fish-hook: 3¼ in.
Width: ¾ in.

BEAD SET UP
Thread on * 6 seed, 2 discs, 1 bead, 2 discs, 6 seed, 1 bead, 2 discs, 1 bead, rep from * twice more.

EARRING (MAKE TWO)
Leave a 4-in. tail end.
Using US 3 needles and wire, cast on 3 sts.
Row 1 (WS): K1B every st to end: (1 bead, 2 discs, 1 bead).

Row 2: P1B every st to end: (6 seed).
Row 3: K1B every st to end: (2 discs, 1 bead, 2 discs).
Row 4: P1B every st to end: (6 seed).
Rep rows 1 to 4 twice more.
Do not bind off.
Leaving a 4-in. tail end, cut wire and sew each st to an end connector hole. Join an earring wire to the single hole of the end connector. Finish off tail ends.

Hearts necklace and earring set

The pretty, red heart-shaped pendants combined with the fine green wire and scattering of tiny, richly colored seed beads give this set a delicate appearance worthy of an expensive price tag. Seed beads are available in a variety of beautiful color mixes and finishes, so this pattern offers you another opportunity to experiment.

✳ Captioned step-by-step pictures on page 70

✳ HOT TIP

Make sure that the brass loops of the heart pendants are tightly closed before use.

The necklace

MATERIALS FOR NECKLACE

- Small spool wire, size 0.20 mm (32 AWG), col green
- 28 x glass heart pendants, size 6 mm, col red with brass loops
- 216 x silver-lined seed beads, size 10/0, col candy mix
- 1 gold lobster clasp
- 12 cm length gold chain
- 1 gold eye pin, length 50 mm
- Pair US 3 knitting needles
- Sewing needle

FINISHED SIZE

Length, excluding findings: 10 in.
Width: 1 in.

BEAD SET UP

Thread on 4 seed, 1 heart, * 8 seed, 1 heart, rep from * until 27 hearts have been threaded onto the wire, ending with 4 seed.

NECKLACE

Leave a 6-in. tail end.
Using US 3 needles and wire, and bringing up a seed bead for each stitch, cast on 5 sts: (4 seed beads worked).
Row 1: Bringing up a heart for first st and seed beads for the other sts, bind off 4 sts. Do not turn. Transfer last st back onto LH needle.
Row 2: Bringing up a seed bead for each st, cast on 4 sts: (5 sts on needle). Rep rows 1 and 2 until all beads have been worked, ending with row 1. Leaving a 6-in. tail end, cut wire and fasten off.

FINISHING

Thread up one tail end onto sewing needle and use to sew the lobster clasp to one end of the necklace. Rep for the other end, sewing the last link of the chain to the necklace. Attach a red heart to the loop of the eye pin. Using pliers, make a loop in the other end of the eye pin, attach it to the last link of the chain, and twist to secure.

① Casting on; putting the 5th stitch onto LH needle.

② Bringing up a heart for 1st stitch.

③ Binding off; knitting seed beads and lifting 1st stitch over second.

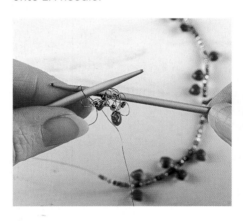

④ Transferring last stitch from RH to LH needle.

⑤ Finishing necklace; sewing on lobster clasp using tail end.

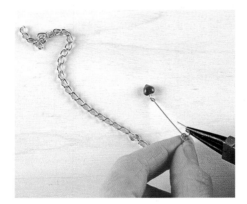

⑥ Finishing necklace; with heart pendant attached, bending eye pin to attach to last link of chain.

⑦ Finishing earring; placing the knotted tail ends into the calotte before closing.

The earrings

MATERIALS FOR TWO EARRINGS

- Small spool wire, size 0.20 mm (32 AWG), col green
- 8 x glass heart pendants, size 6 mm, col red with brass loops
- 64 x silver-lined seed beads, size 10/0, col candy mix
- 2 gold calottes
- 2 gold fish-hook earring wires
- Pair US 3 knitting needles
- Sewing needle

FINISHED SIZE

Length, to bend of fish-hook: 2½ in.
Width: ¾ in.

BEAD SET UP

Thread on 4 seed, * 1 heart, 8 seed, rep from * until 4 hearts have been threaded onto the wire, ending with 4 seed.

EARRING (MAKE TWO)

Leave a 3¼-in. tail end.
Using US 3 needles and wire, and bringing up a seed bead for each stitch, cast on 5 sts: (4 seed beads worked).
Row 1: Bringing up a heart for first st and seed beads for the other sts, bind off 4sts. Do not turn. Transfer last st back onto LH needle.
Row 2: Bringing up a seed bead for each st, cast on 4 sts: (5 sts on needle).
Rep rows 1 and 2 once more, then rep row 1 again.
Do not transfer last st, turn.
Rep row 2, then row 1.
Next row: Cast on 1 st.
Next row: K2tog.
Leaving an 3¼-in. tail end, cut wire and fasten off.

FINISHING

Twist last tail ends to form a knot. Place knot in a calotte and squeeze gently to close. Join a fish-hook earring wire to the calotte. Neaten other tail end.

Glass pendant choker and wristband

Small iridescent pendant beads make a lovely statement when they are knitted in simple rows. The finely knitted, stockinette stitch wire mesh produces a delicate backdrop to these simple pieces. These beads are available in many colors, creating opportunities to try different combinations. Once the beads are threaded, the actual knitting is relatively straightforward.

★ Captioned step-by-step pictures on page 74

The choker

MATERIALS FOR CHOKER
- Small spool wire, size 0.20 mm (32 AWG), col light gold
- 351 x glass pendants, size 4 x 6 mm, col light green
- 2 gold end connectors (7 holes on one side and 1 hole on the other), width 35 mm
- 1 gold lobster clasp
- 7 mm gold jump ring
- 5 mm gold jump ring
- 10 cm length of gold chain
- Pair US 3 knitting needles
- Sewing needle

FINISHED SIZE
Length, excluding findings: 10 in.
Width: 2¼ in.

BEAD SET UP
Thread on 351 beads.

CHOKER
Leave a 4¾-in. tail end.

Using US 3 needles and wire, cast on 11 sts.
Row 1 (WS): K1B, * k1, k1B, rep from * to end: (6 beads worked).
Row 2 and every RS row: K1B, p to end: (1 bead worked).
Row 3: K1, * k1B, k1, rep from * to end: (5 beads worked).
Row 4: As row 2.
Rep rows 1 to 4 another 26 times: (108 rows have been worked).
Bind off loosely.
Leaving a 4¾-in. tail end, cut wire and fasten off.

FINISHING
Join the lobster clasp to one of the end connectors with the 5 mm jump ring. Thread one of the tail ends onto sewing needle and sew the connector holes to the end of the choker. Join the other connector to the length of chain with the 7 mm jump ring and sew to the other end of the choker. Finish off tail ends and trim close to work.

▷

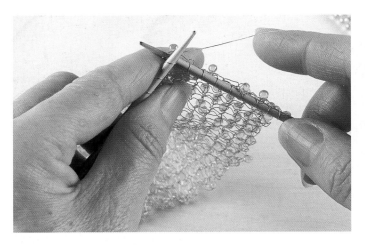

1 *K1B; wrapping wire knitwise with pendant in place.*

2 *Purling on RS rows; preparing to wrap wire.*

3 *Sewing on an end connector with lobster clasp attached.*

4 *Attaching chain to an end connector with a jump ring.*

5 *Sewing on clasp using tail end, keeping the stitches loose.*

6 *Winding the remaining tail end around the shank.*

The wristband

MATERIALS FOR WRISTBAND
- Small spool wire, size 0.20 mm (32 AWG), col black
- 198 x glass pendants, size 4 x 6 mm, col red
- 1 toggle clasp, size 10 mm clasp and 20 mm toggle, col bronze
- Pair US 3 knitting needles
- Sewing needle

FINISHED SIZE
Length, including findings: 7 in.
Width: 1¾-in.

BEAD SET UP
Thread 198 beads onto wire.

WRISTBAND
Leave a 4¾-in. tail end.
Using US 3 needles and wire, cast on 9 sts.
Row 1 (WS): K1B, * k1, k1B, rep from * to end: (5 beads worked).
Row 2 and every RS row: K1B, p to end: (1 bead worked).
Row 3: K1, * k1B, k1, rep from * to end: (4 beads worked).
Row 4: As row 2.
Rep rows 1 to 4 another 17 times: (72 rows have been worked).
Bind off loosely.
Leaving a 4¾-in. tail end, cut wire and fasten off.

FINISHING
Weave tail end through to center of bound-off end. Keeping stitches loose, thread through connector hole of toggle and knitting a few times to secure. Rep for cast-on end, joining to the connector hole of clasp. Wind tail ends around shanks to finish. Trim wire close to work.

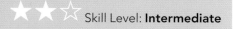

Sequin and multibead choker

There are some wonderful glass beads available in premixed packs, and none are more striking than the iridescent (AB) faceted bead selection used in this choker. To achieve the luxury and depth of this glamorous piece, different sizes and colors of glass beads have been alternated with seed beads and gold discs, which partially conceal the beads and act as mirrors to reflect the overall sparkle.

✳ Captioned step-by-step pictures on page 78

✳ HOT TIP
To ensure an even spread when threading beads, prepare dishes of beads according to size. To keep a balance, it is important that the larger beads are distributed evenly.

✳ SPECIAL INSTRUCTIONS
Bringing up a bead after a slip stitch (sl.1) allows the bead to lie on the right side of a knit row. Hold the bead at the front of the work with your thumb to avoid the bead moving to the wrong side of the work when you take the yarn back for the knit stitch.

The choker

MATERIALS
• Small spool wire, size 0.20 mm (32 AWG), col gun bronze
• 81 x discs, size15 mm, col gold
• 329 x color-lined seed beads, size 10/0, col pink
• 80 x glass bead selection
• Medium gold lobster clasp
• 5 mm gold jump ring
• 9 mm gold jump ring
• 2 gold end connectors (7 holes on one side and 1 hole on the other), width 35 mm
• 4-in. length of gold chain
• Pair US 7 knitting needles
• Sewing needle

FINISHED SIZE
Length, excluding findings: 11 in.
Width: 1½ in.

BEAD SET UP
Thread on 47 seed, * 1 disc, (1 bead, 1 disc) 11 times, 47 seed, 1 bead (1 disc, 1 bead) 11 times, 47 seed, rep from * twice more, ending 1 disc (1 bead, 1 disc) 11 times.

CHOKER
Leave a 6-in. tail end.
Using US 7 needles and wire, cast on 47 sts.
Row 1 (RS): K1, * yfwd, sl.1, bring up a disc or bead, ybk, k1, rep from * to end: (23 discs or beads).
Row 2: K1B to end: (47 seed beads).
Rep rows 1 and 2 until 13 rows have been completed.
Bringing up a seed bead for each st, bind off loosely.
Leaving a 6-in. tail end, cut wire and fasten off.

FINISHING
Join the lobster clasp to one of the end connectors with the 5 mm jump ring. Thread one of the tail ends onto sewing needle and sew the connector holes to the end of the choker. Join the other connector to the length of chain with the 9 mm jump ring and sew to the other end of the choker. Finish off tail ends and trim close to work.

▷

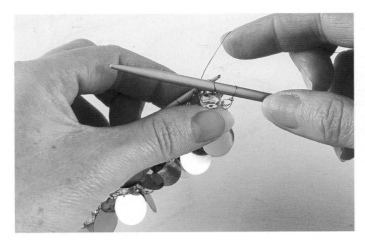

① *Sl.1 with a bead; taking ybk, bead is in place ready for knitting next stitch.*

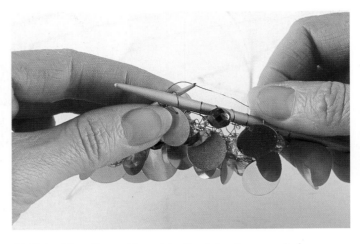

② *Sl.1 with a disc; taking ybk, disc is in place ready for knitting next stitch.*

③ *K1B; wrapping wire knitwise with seed bead in place.*

④ *Binding off with seed beads; lifting first stitch over second.*

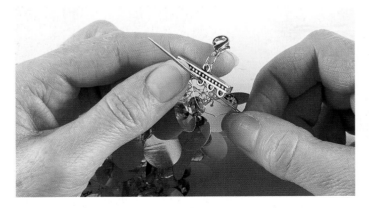

⑤ *Sewing on an end connector with lobster clasp attached.*

⑥ *Attaching chain to an end connector with a jump ring.*

Chunky glass wristbands

These wristbands have a touch of the medieval about them. The pattern is not difficult, but the thickness of the wire takes a little getting used to. The main project features pink tubes, with variations made using heart-shaped glass beads. All the wristbands are fastened with uncluttered toggle sets.

★ Captioned step-by-step pictures on page 82

★ Captioned step-by-step pictures on page 82

★ HOT TIP
Because the wire is very stiff, it is not necessary to use a sewing needle for attaching the findings or darning in the tail ends.

★ SPECIAL INSTRUCTIONS
Sl.5P: Keeping wire at the front of the work, slip the next 5 sts without knitting them.

Wristband with pink tubes

MATERIALS FOR WRISTBAND WITH PINK TUBES
• Small spool wire, size 0.50 mm (24 AWG), col black
• 5 x 28mm silver-lined glass tubes, col pink
• 2 toggle clasps, size 10 mm clasp and 20 mm toggle, col bronze
• Pair US 7 knitting needles

FINISHED SIZE
Length, including findings: 7-in.
Width: 2½ in.

BEAD SET UP
Thread 5 pink tubes onto the wire.

WRISTBAND WITH PINK TUBES
Leave a 8-in. tail end.
Using US 7 needles and wire, cast on 7 sts.
Row 1 (RS): K.

Row 2: K1, p5, k1.
Rows 3 to 6: Rep rows 1 and 2 twice more.
Row 7: K1, yfwd, bringing up a bead, sl.5P, ybk, k1.
Row 8: As row 2.
Rep rows 3 to 8 four times more.
Rep rows 1 and 2 three times more.
Bind off very loosely.
Leaving a 8-in. tail end, cut wire and fasten off.

FINISHING
Using a pair of round-nose pliers, twist wire at bottom of each bead to secure. Weave tail end through bound-off end of knitting to third of way along. Keeping the stitches on the loose side, thread though connector hole of toggle and the knitting a few times to secure. Wind wire around shank before weaving tail end along a third more to join next toggle. Wind tail end around shank to finish off. Trim wire close to work. Rep for cast-on end, joining to the connector hole of each clasp.

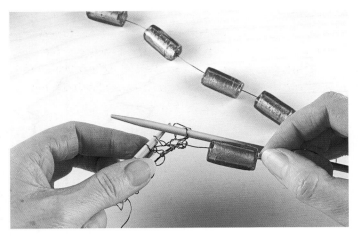

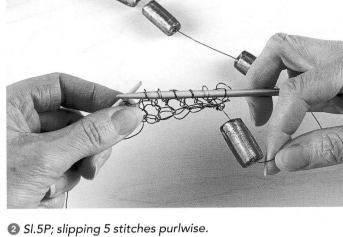

① Yfwd, bringing up a bead.

② Sl.5P; slipping 5 stitches purlwise.

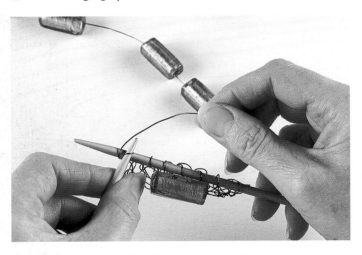

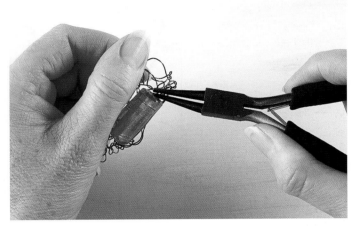

③ Ybk, keeping bead in place at front of the work, preparing to knit next stitch.

④ Twisting the wire, holding the bead to secure in place.

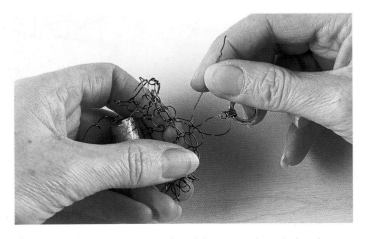

⑤ Sewing on clasp using tail end, keeping the stitches loose.

⑥ Winding the remaining tail end around the shank.

Wristband with pink heart

MATERIALS FOR SILVER WRISTBAND WITH PINK HEART

- Small spool wire, size 0.50 mm (24 AWG), col silver plated
- 2 x 28 mm silver-lined glass heart, col crystal
- 1 x 28 mm silver-lined glass hearts, col pink
- Toggle clasp, size16 mm clasp and 22 mm toggle, col silver
- Pair US 7 knitting needles

FINISHED SIZE

Length, including findings: 7½ in.
Width: 2½ in.

BEAD SET UP

With all hearts facing same way, thread on 1 crystal, 1 pink, 1 crystal.

WRISTBAND WITH PINK HEART

Leave a 7-in. tail end.
Using US 7 needles and wire, cast on 7 sts.
Row 1 (RS): K.
Row 2: K1, p5, k1.
Rows 3–8: Rep rows 1 and 2 three times more.
Row 9: K1, yfwd, bringing up a bead, sl.5P, ybk, k1.
Row 10: As row 2.
Rep rows 1 to 10 twice more.
Rep rows 1 and 2 four times more.
Bind off very loosely.
Leaving a 7-in. tail end, cut wire and fasten off.

FINISHING

Using a pair of round-nose pliers, twist wire at bottom of each bead to secure. Weave tail end through to center of bound-off end. Keeping stitches loose, thread through connector hole of toggle and the knitting a few times to secure. Rep for cast-on end, joining to the connector hole of the clasp. Wind tail ends around shanks to finish off. Trim wire close to work.

Wristband with green and brown hearts

MATERIALS FOR WRISTBAND WITH GREEN AND BROWN HEARTS

- Small spool wire, size 0.50 mm (24 AWG), col black
- 2 x 28 mm silver-lined glass hearts, col green
- 1 x 28 mm silver-lined glass heart, col brown
- 2 toggle clasps, size 10 mm clasp and 20 mm toggle, col bronze
- Pair US 7 knitting needles

FINISHED SIZE

Length, including findings: 7½ in.
Width: 2½ in.

BEAD SET UP

With all hearts facing the same way, thread on 1 green, 1 brown, 1 green.

WRISTBAND WITH GREEN AND BROWN HEARTS

Leave a 8-in. tail end.
Using US 7 needles and wire, cast on 7 sts.
Row 1 (RS): K.
Row 2: K1, p5, k1.
Rows 3–8: Rep rows 1 and 2 three times more.
Row 9: K1, yfwd, bringing up a bead, sl.5P, ybk, k1.
Row 10: As row 2.
Rep rows 1 to 10 twice more.
Rep rows 1 and 2 four times more.
Bind off very loosely.
Leaving a 8-in. tail end, cut wire and fasten off.

FINISHING

Using a pair of round-nose pliers, twist wire at bottom of each bead to secure. Weave tail end through bound-off end of knitting to third of way along. Keeping the stitches on the loose side, thread through connector hole of toggle and the knitting a few times to secure. Wind wire around shank before weaving tail end along a third more to join next toggle. Wind tail end around shank to neaten. Trim wire close to work. Rep for cast-on end, joining to the connector hole of each clasp.

Multistrand necklace and earring set

This stunning set is made from combining tiny crystal and pink seed beads with a mixture of leaf-shaped, heart-shaped, faceted, and round beads with different finishes. Follow the list of beads given below to create this subtle pink combination, or use some of the fabulous premixed bags available from many bead outlets and suppliers.

★ Captioned step-by-step pictures on pages 88–89

★ HOT TIP
Prepare three saucers for the beads; one each for the two seed bead colors and a larger plate to mix the other bead combinations.

★ SPECIAL INSTRUCTIONS
The mixed beads are worked singly and the seed beads are worked in pairs throughout.

When threading the seed beads, alternate the two colors and thread the other mixed beads randomly. When casting on with beads, note that the slip knot is not beaded.

The necklace

MATERIALS FOR NECKLACE
- Small spool wire, size 0.20 mm (32 AWG), col silver plated

Beaded strands
- 156 x bead mix, containing the following:
- Matt glass leaves, size 11 x 7 mm, col pink AB
- Matt glass leaves, size 3 x 11 mm, col pink AB
- Matt glass hearts, size 6 mm, col pink AB
- Matt glass round beads, size 4 mm, col pink AB
- Half-coated faceted glass beads, size 4 mm, col rose
- Faceted glass beads, size 6 mm and 4 mm, col crystal AB
- Faceted glass beads, size 6 mm, col pink AB
- Square glass beads, size 5 x 6 mm, col crystal AB
- Glass pendant, size 4 x 6 mm, col crystal AB
- 168 x pearlized seed beads, size 10/0, col pink
- 168 x transparent seed beads, size 10/0, col crystal

Necklace
- 2 x faceted glass beads, size 6 mm, col crystal AB
- 206 x pearlized seed beads, size 10/0, col pink
- 208 x transparent seed beads, size 10/0, col crystal
- 1 silver lobster clasp
- 9mm silver jump ring
- Pair US 3 knitting needles
- Sewing needle
- 12 safety pins

FINISHED SIZE
Length, including findings: 15½ in.
Width at center point: 4 in.

▷

NECKLACE STRANDS

4-stitch strand (Make 2)

Bead Set Up

Thread on 2 seed, * 1 mix, 2 seed, rep from * twice more.

Using US 3 needles and wire, bringing up beads as set for each stitch, cast on 4 sts. Turn.

Bringing up beads as set for each stitch, bind off 4 sts. Cut wire and leave last st on a safety pin.

8-stitch strand (Make 2)

Bead Set Up

Thread on 2 seed, * 1 mix, 2 seed, rep from * 6 times more.

Using US 3 needles and wire, bringing up beads as set for each stitch, cast on 8 sts. Turn.

Bringing up beads as set for each stitch, bind off 8 sts. Cut wire and leave last st on a safety pin.

12-stitch strand (Make 2)

Bead Set Up

Thread on 2 seed, * 1 mix, 2 seed, rep from * 10 times more.

Using US 3 needles and wire, bringing up beads as set for each stitch, cast on 12 sts. Turn.

Bringing up beads as set for each stitch, bind off 12 sts. Cut wire and leave last st on a safety pin.

16-stitch strand (Make 2)

Bead Set Up

Thread on 2 seed, * 1 mix, 2 seed, rep from * 14 times more.

Using US 3 needles and wire, bringing up beads as set for each stitch, cast on 16 sts. Turn.

Bringing up beads as set for each stitch, bind off 16 sts. Cut wire and leave last st on a safety pin.

20-stitch strand (Make 2)

Bead Set Up

Thread on 2 seed, * 1 mix, 2 seed, rep from * 18 times more.

Using US 3 needles and wire, bringing up beads as set for each stitch, cast on 20 sts. Turn.

Bringing up beads as set for each stitch, bind off 20 sts. Cut wire and leave last st on a safety pin.

24-stitch strand (Make 2)

Bead Set Up

Thread on 2 seed, * 1 mix, 2 seed, rep from * 22 times more.

Using US 3 needles and wire, bringing up beads as set for each stitch, cast on 24 sts. Turn.

Bringing up beads as set for each stitch, bind off 24 sts. Cut wire and leave last st on a safety pin.

NECKLACE

Bead Set Up

Thread onto wire 414 seed beads as follows:

* 2 crystal, 2 pink, rep from * until all the seed beads have been threaded, ending 2 crystal.

Using US 3 needles and wire, bringing up 2 seed beads as set for each stitch, cast on 38 sts.

Now work across all the bead strands as follows:

Arrange the 12 bead strands in order from 4 st to 24 st and from 24 st back to 4 st.

Inserting RH needle into last st of the first bead strand, draw through a st. Now bringing up 2 seed beads as before, cast on 2 sts. * Insert RH needle into last st of next-size bead strand and draw through a loop. Then, bringing up 2 seed beads for each st, cast on

2 sts, rep from * until all bead strands have been attached, then bringing up 2 seed beads for each st, cast on a further 38 sts: (110 sts).

Bringing up 2 seed beads for each st, bind off all sts.

Leaving a 4-in. tail end, cut wire and fasten off.

FINISHING

Fasten off all bead strand tail ends, securing each join in the process. Trim close to work.

Thread necklace tail ends through one of the 6 mm faceted glass beads, the lobster clasp, and back through the glass bead. Rep to secure and fasten off. Trim close to work. Rep for other end, joining in wire for tail end and sewing to the remaining glass bead and the 9 mm jump ring.

❶ Sorting beads into sets before threading onto the wire.

❷ Casting on with beads; putting the stitch onto LH needle.

❸ Binding off with beads; lifting first stitch over second.

❹ Joining on strands to necklace; pulling a loop through last stitch of strand to make the next stitch.

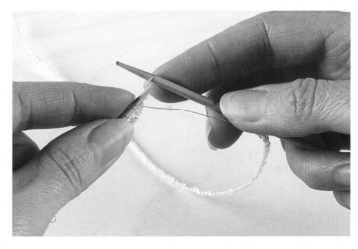

❺ Make necklace band: casting on with seed beads; putting the stitch onto LH needle.

❻ All strands attached with 110 stitches on needle; preparing to bind off. The tail ends are undarned.

❼ Binding off stitches over the strands; bringing up two seed beads for each stitch to finish the necklace band.

❽ Finishing necklace; threading tail end through glass bead and lobster clasp before darning off.

⑨ *Finishing earring; sewing a strand to an end connector.*

⑩ *Finishing earring; closing connector loop of earring wire.*

The earrings

MATERIALS FOR EARRINGS
- Small spool wire, size 0.20 mm (32 AWG), col silver plated
- 90 x bead mix as for necklace
- 96 x pearlized seed beads, size 10/0, col pink
- 96 x transparent seed beads, size 10/0, col crystal
- 2 silver fish-hook earring wires
- 2 silver end connectors (3 holes on one side and 1 hole on the other), width 12 mm
- Pair US 3 knitting needles
- Sewing needle

FINISHED SIZE
Length, to bend of fish-hook: 3½ in.
Width: ¾ in.

EARRING STRANDS
16-stitch strand (make 3 per earring)
Bead Set Up

Thread on 2 seed, * 1 mix, 2 seed, rep from * 14 times more.
Leave a 2-in. tail end.
Using US 3 needles and wire, bringing up beads as set for each stitch, cast on 16 sts. Turn.
Bringing up beads as set for each stitch, bind off 16 sts.
Leaving a 2-in. tail end, cut wire and fasten off.

FINISHING
Thread up tail ends of one beaded strand onto sewing needle and sew to one of the three end connector holes. Repeat for the other two strands. Neaten off all tail ends and trim close to work.
Using flat-nosed pliers, carefully open connector loop of earring wire and join to single hole of end connector. Close securely.

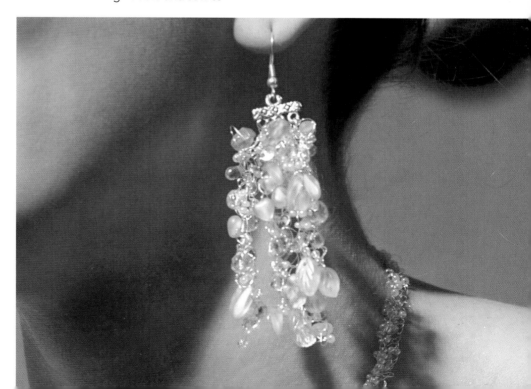

★★★ Skill level: **Advanced**

Small Aran bag

If you want to venture into "fully fashioned" knitting, the pattern for this bag is a little gem. Follow the instructions carefully and you will learn useful shaping and sewing techniques to introduce you to good habits, which will give your work a really professional finish. To help you concentrate on knitting correctly, the beads are sewn on before the bag is sewn together.

✳ Captioned step-by-step pictures on page 93–95

✳ HOT TIP

Make sure that the cable needle is the same size or slightly smaller than the knitting needles. In this way, you will avoid stretching the stitches as you turn the cables.

✳ SPECIAL INSTRUCTIONS

It is difficult to create a neat seam when a seed stitch pattern is taken right to the end of each row. To overcome this problem, and to create a frame for the cable pattern, each row of the pattern begins and ends with st.st. This allows the shaping to be worked inside the st.st band and the side seams to be sewn using mattress stitch. The resulting seams will be flat and, if sewn carefully, invisible.

The bag

MATERIALS FOR BAG

- 2 x 1¾ oz. balls Aran cotton yarn, col denim blue
- Beads (assuming both sides of bag are beaded)
- 10 x silver-lined glass discs, size 12 mm, col gray
- 26 x crackle finish glass beads, size 8 mm, col fushia pink
- 58 x faceted glass beads, size 6 mm, col AB pink
- 108 x opaque seed beads, size 10/0, col light green
- Pair US 7 knitting needles
- Pair US 6 knitting needles
- Medium-sized cable needle
- 4 safety pins
- Fine beading needle
- Darning needle
- Knitter's needle
- Sewing thread

FINISHED SIZE

Length, including handle: 8¾ in.
Width at widest point: 9 in.

BAG

Back and front (both alike)

Leave a 20 cm tail end.

Using 4½ mm needles and cotton yarn, cast on 34 sts.

Row 1 (RS): K3, (p1, k1) 5 times, p2, k4, p2, (k1, p1) 5 times, k3.

Row 2: P3, (k1, p1) 5 times, k2, p4, k2, (p1, k1) 5 times, p3.

Row 3: K3, M1P, (k1, p1) 5 times, p1, T3B, T3F, p1, (p1, k1) 5 times, M1P, k3.

Row 4: P3, M1P, (k1, p1) 5 times, k2, (p2, k2) twice, (p1, k1) 5 times, M1P, p3.

Row 5: K3, M1K, (p1, k1) 5 times, p2, T3B, p2, T3F, p2, (k1, p1) 5 times, M1K, k3.

Row 6: P3, M1K, (p1, k1) 6 times, k1, p2, k4, p2, k1, (k1, p1) 6 times, M1K, p3.

Row 7: K3, M1P, (k1, p1) 6 times, p1, T3B, p4, T3F, p1, (p1, k1) 6 times, M1P, k3.

Row 8: P3, M1P, (k1, p1) 6 times, k2, p2, k6, p2, k2, (p1, k1) 6 times, M1P, p3.

Row 9: K3, M1K, (p1, k1) 6 times, p2, T3B, p6, T3F, p2, (k1, p1) 6 times, M1K, k3.

Row 10: P3, M1K, (p1, k1) 7 times, k1, p2, k8, p2, k1, (k1, p1) 7 times, M1K, p3.

Row 11: K3, M1P, (k1, p1) 7 times, p1, T3B, p8, T3F, p1, (p1, k1) 7 times, M1P, k3: (52 sts).

Row 12: P3, (k1, p1) 7 times, k2, p2, k10, p2, k2, (p1, k1) 7 times, p3.

Row 13: K3, (k1, p1) 7 times, p1, T3B, p10, T3F, p1, (p1, k1) 7 times, k3.

Row 14: P3, (p1, k1) 7 times, k1, p2, k12, p2, k1, (k1, p1) 7 times, p3.

Row 15: K3, (p1, k1) 6 times, p2, T3B, p12, T3F, p2, (k1, p1) 6 times, k3.

Row 16: P3, (k1, p1) 6 times, k2, p2, k14, p2, k2, (p1, k1) 6 times, p3.

Row 17: K2, skp, (p1, k1) 5 times, p2, T3B, p14, T3F, p2, (k1, p1) 5 times, K2tog, k2.

Row 18: P3, (k1, p1) 5 times, k2, p2, k16, p2, k2, (p1, k1) 5 times, p3.

Row 19: K2, skp, (p1, k1) 4 times, p2, T3B, p16, T3F, p2, (k1, p1) 4 times, k2tog, k2.

Row 20: P3, (k1, p1) 4 times, k2, p2, k18, p2, k2, (p1, k1) 4 times, p3.

Row 21: K2, skp, (p1, k1) 4 times, p1, T3F, p16, T3B, p1, (k1, p1) 4 times, k2tog, k2.

Row 22: P3, (k1, p1) 4 times, k2, p2, k16, p2, k2, (p1, k1) 4 times, p3.

Row 23: K2, skp, (p1, k1) 4 times, p1, T3F, p14, T3B, p1, (k1, p1) 4 times, k2tog, k2.

Row 24: P3, (k1, p1) 4 times, k2, p2, k14, p2, k2, (p1, k1) 4 times, p3.

Row 25: K2, skp, (p1, k1) 4 times, p1, T3F, p12, T3B, p1, (k1, p1) 4 times, k2tog, k2.

Row 26: P3, (k1, p1) 4 times, k2, p2, k12, p2, k2, (p1, k1) 4 times, p3.

Row 27: K2, skp, (p1, k1) 4 times, p1, T3F, p10, T3B, p1, (k1, p1) 4 times, k2tog, k2.

Row 28: P3, (k1, p1) 4 times, k2, p2, k10, p2, k2, (p1, k1) 4 times, p3.

Row 29: K2, skp, (p1, k1) 4 times, p1, T3F, p8, T3B, p1, (k1, p1) 4 times, k2tog, k2.

Row 30: P3, (k1, p1) 4 times, k2, p2, k8, p2, k2, (p1, k1) 4 times, p3.

Row 31: K2, skp, (p1, k1) 4 times, p1, T3F, p6, T3B, p1, (k1, p1) 4 times, k2tog, k2.

Row 32: P3, (k1, p1) 4 times, k2, p2, k6, p2, k2, (p1, k1) 4 times, p3.

Row 33: K2, skp, (p1, k1) 4 times, p1, T3F, p4, T3B, p1, (k1, p1) 4 times, k2tog, k2.

Row 34: P3, (k1, p1) 4 times, k2, p2, k4, p2, k2, (p1, k1) 4 times, p3.

Row 35: K2, skp, (p1, k1) 4 times, p1, T3F, p2, T3B, p1, (k1, p1) 4 times, k2tog, k2.

Row 36: P3, (k1, p1) 4 times, (k2, p2) twice, k2, (k1, p1) 4 times, p3.

Row 37: K2, skp, (p1, k1) 4 times, p1, T3F, T3B, p1, (k1, p1) 4 times, k2tog, k2.

Row 38: P3, (k1, p1) 4 times, k2, p4, k2, (p1, k1) 4 times, p3: (30 sts).

Make stitches for handle:

Row 39: K4, (kfb into next stitch) 4 times, k14, (kfb into next stitch) 4 times, k4: (38 sts).

Row 40: K4, (k1, slip next st onto a safety pin and leave on RS of work) 4 times, k14, (k1, slip next st onto a holder) 4 times, k4.

Row 41: Bind off 30 sts on needle.

Make handle

With RS of work facing, slip stitches from RH safety pin onto a US 6 needle. Rejoin yarn to first stitch and knit 4 sts. Starting with a p row, work in st.st until handle measures 6¾ in., ending with a p row.

Leaving a 12-in. tail end, break yarn. Thread tail end onto a knitter's needle. Graft sts to 4 sts on LH safety pin as follows:

Insert needle from back to front of first st on knitting needle and pull yarn through.

Insert needle from back to front of first st on holder and pull yarn through.

Insert needle from front to back of first st and back to front of second st on knitting needle.

Insert needle from front to back of first st and back to front of second st on safety pin.

Rep in this way with second and third stitches and third and fourth stitches. Break yarn and adjust all grafted sts to tension.

FINISHING

Darn off tail ends for handles.

Using a fine beading needle threaded with sewing thread, sew on beads, using the chart on page 95 as a guide.

Starting at bottom edge, sew right hand seam using mattress stitch, then sew cast-on stitches using oversew stitch and complete LH seam using mattress stitch.

Darn in rem tail ends on the WS and trim close to work.

① M1; preparing to knit into back of stitch.

② M1P; preparing to purl into back of stitch.

③ T3B; holding stitch at back of work and knitting second stitch from LH needle.

④ T3B; preparing to purl stitch from CN.

⑤ T3F; holding 2 stitches at front of and purling next stitch from LH needle.

⑥ T3F; knitting second stitch from CN.

▷

7 *Skp; passing the slipped stitch over knitted stitch to decrease a stitch.*

8 *K2tog; inserting RH needle into next two stitches from left to right and preparing to knit the stitch.*

9 *Make stitches for handle, row 39 Kfb; knitting into front of stitch, but not taking the stitch off LH needle.*

10 *Kfb; inserting needle into back of same stitch and preparing to knit stitch. Continue by taking stitches off LH needle.*

11 *Make stitches for handle, row 40; slipping a stitch onto a safety pin after knitting a stitch and leaving on RS of work.*

12 *Grafting stitches; inserting needle from front to back of first stitch and back to front of second stitch on knitting needle.*

⓭ *Grafting stitches; inserting needle from front to back of first stitch and back to front of second stitch on holder.*

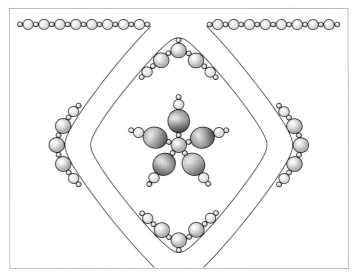

⓮ *Sewing on beads.*

KEY TO CHART

○ Seed beads, opaque green

⬤ SL glass discs, 12 mm gray

○ Crackle finish, 8 mm fushia

○ Faceted glass bead, 6 mm AB pink

⓯ *Mattress stitch; inserting needle into first stitch and out of the second stitch, repeating for second side.*

⓰ *Oversew stitch; inserting needle into cast on stitches for both pieces, yarn is carried over the top of work.*

Index and Acknowledgments

ACKNOWLEDGMENTS

Firstly, I'd like to thank Rosemary Wilkinson and her great team, Naomi and Lisa, for making this possible. Thank you again Shona for your patience and eye for detail during the step-by-step photography. And thank you Paul and the three models for the lovely outdoor photography of the finished pieces.

As always, my students at South Thames College inspire me. It's a real pleasure to teach you all—keep up the passion for knitting! My knitting friends: Sarah, Trish, Sue, Ruth, and Fiona for their help trawling through the proofs and for their invaluable feedback. Finally, to my family, thank you Mark for taking the children to the skate park to give me some space.